DECORATING MAGIC

DECORATING MAGIC

John Sutcliffe

Pantheon Books, New York

This book is for Gabrielle, with love

Conceived, edited and designed by Frances Lincoln Limited,
Apollo Works, 5 Charlton King's Road, London NW5 2SB, England.

Published in the United States by Pantheon Books, a division of Random House, Inc., New York.

Library of Congress Cataloging-in-Publication Data
Sutcliffe, John.
     Decorating magic / John Sutcliffe.
        p.   cm.
     Includes index.
     ISBN 0-679-41212-3
        1. Interior decoration – Handbooks, manuals, etc.   I. Title.
     NK2115.S88   1992
     747—dc20
                                                          91–42667
                                                          CIP

Printed and bound in Great Britain by Butler & Tanner Limited

First American edition

CONTENTS

INTRODUCTION

Decorating Magic provides a craftsman's approach to decoration. The book explores what it is that makes certain interiors successful by considering the overall concept that lies behind their design and examining the details of their execution.

The art of good decorating is to conceal itself. There should be a sense of inevitability – which does not rule out shock tactics – about the way a room looks, a reason behind each choice in decoration. When a room is completed, there should be no regrets about any aspect of its design and execution, and it should be impossible to imagine the room having been treated in any other way. To the craftsman, any finish – whether in paint or paper, wood or cloth – is subservient to the effect he or she wants to create, not an end in itself.

To focus attention on the overall design, *Decorating Magic* is organized not conventionally by technique but instead by type of decoration, so that the emphasis properly falls first where it belongs, on the rooms and their surfaces, and only secondly on materials and techniques. The book's chapters are arranged to represent a series of types of room. The categories chosen for the chapters refer to the qualities that most markedly put their stamp on the final appearance of an interior. This is a deliberately personal list of criteria, and I have worked on many of the rooms illustrated and completely designed and executed some of them. The chapters do not, of course, form watertight compartments: rooms may exhibit several qualities at once, and the same technique may be used in different room 'types'. For example, marbling, as a paint finish producing the effect of natural stone, belongs, in one sense, to the Stony Room, but since they can also be used to create a pattern, marbling techniques are equally relevant to the Patterned Room.

There has been an explosion of interest over the past decade in what are generally termed 'paint effects', of which marbling is one example. While using such effects is a way of signalling that care and attention have been expended on a surface, it is of paramount importance to see them in context and consider their contribution to the room. A well-prepared, well-executed ragrolled wall can be a beautiful thing in itself, but while ragrolling a wall may show care and give an illusion of choice, it will not, by itself, hide a lack of conceptual finesse. Good technique alone is no substitute for a carefully devised approach that takes the whole scheme for the room into account. And although paint is a tremendously satisfying material to use, and one that seems almost infinitely versatile, it is not merely by mastering paint effects that one creates a successful room. A room's proportions and details, the amount of light it receives, how it is to be used and, of course, personal preference, are all relevant when devising a scheme for its decoration. And storage and display, paper and cloth, pictures and fittings will all

Any successful room will exhibit more than one of the elements featured in this book, while holding them in some kind of balance. This room is lined with early-eighteenth-century panelling – with its characteristic vertical emphasis – and is painted in a stylized monochrome marbling. The sense of enclosure created by the panelling is balanced by the cool colourlessness of stone. Pattern, already present in the rhythmical marbling, is further introduced in the tabletop which is done in marbled wallpaper, cut and intricately joined and varnished.

The walls are cool in tone and verge towards green. To give the room a warm sparkle the chairs and picture frames and the chintz bag covering the chandelier chain are in complementary red; since these areas are small (and the grey and green areas large) the red is bright and has fine white lines to crispen it.

There is a concentration of white in the china plates and tureen – putting the focus where it belongs.

play their part in helping the room to make a statement.

Part of the popular appeal of paint effects has been the notion of rediscovering 'authentic' materials and arcane skills and so achieving historically accurate results. We may get a frisson of excitement from the knowledge that our paints contain dangerous lead, that our distemper will rub off on our clothes and hands, that our wallpapers contain enough arsenic to kill an Emperor, but we must ask whether any real visual benefits are to be gained from the use of these materials. It is important to understand why decorating techniques were invented in the first place and the reasons for their evolution and development. Just as the value of a technique when isolated from the purpose for which it is used has to be questioned, so does the notion of 'authenticity at all costs'.

Apart from its romantic feel, certain aspects of 'authenticity' have unique aesthetic qualities that must commend themselves to us. Distemper, for example, cheap, easy to apply and now readily available again, has a wonderfully dry, powdery look and can be strengthened with a little latex glaze so that it does not come off to the touch. Flatting coats on oil paint have an unparalleled translucency and subtlety when used as a finish, and handblocked distemper-printed wallpapers in their directness and actual depth have a quality which 'authentic reproductions' fail to achieve. But complete authenticity, even if it could be achieved, is not usually desirable, given our wish for the convenience and comfort of modern living. However, once this is accepted, the past can be used fruitfully as a mine of inspiration rather than being mindlessly rendered in reproduction.

There is much to be said in favour of traditional approaches when used in this light. After all, many of the old techniques – even those that may appear complicated – were carried out with ordinary, everyday tools and materials by craftsmen who simply had time to perfect their dexterity with uncomplicated ingredients. Limited resources can prove a positive advantage and will form an automatic check to over-elaboration. The directness of working methods of many old techniques has an immediate appeal of its own.

The real point of adopting historical precedents is to keep traditions alive, and traditions evolve and change. The great English decorator, John Fowler, did not seek to create strictly 'authentic' interiors, but his schemes for period houses were highly successful. Very much aware of historical precedent and deeply knowledgeable, he was able to contribute a further inspired layer, to take a sideways jump and invigorate interiors which might otherwise have become lifeless under the weight of too rigorously academic an approach. Some of his schemes were controversial and to purists even offensive, but his detractors would have to admit that Fowler put the personal experience of his rooms back at the centre of things. The rooms were seen as a whole; historical details, lovingly and knowledgeably applied were made to fit the vision.

Much of what we admire about old houses, and what serves as a source of ideas about what is 'authentic' has come about because of the passage of time. The signs of wear and use in themselves are appealing. This can be achieved through the re-use of old materials or by 'distressing' to simulate age. Fowler, sympathetic to the notion of 'distressing', also relied on soft colours and subtle shades of white to help blend old and new.

In the same spirit, *Decorating Magic* is concerned to provide a background against which to make informed choices. As well as taking the wide view, the book focuses on minutiae, for details and care in execution are what make a room successful once the basic concept has been established. Through reference to historical precedent and specially prepared examples, it helps to put the skills described in technical manuals into useful perspective and to redirect them towards achieving the desired results – even occasionally going into some detail to correct oversimplification in other sources. The idea is to demonstrate how, if we understand the reasons for techniques and materials, we can use them to create harmonious rooms which display the proper level of care and finish. In the end, the result must be a room which you enjoy and which, however complicated or simple it may be, gives pleasure in every part.

John Sutcliffe

THE COLOURED ROOM

Colour, skilfully used, can transform a dark or even featureless interior. The distinctly old-fashioned colours on this stairway – Pompeiian red, earthy grey, black and gold – are evocative as well as practical. The deeply distressed red earth colour summons up images of crumbling Italian colourwashed walls. Here, though, it has been applied in a varnished oil glaze, both for practicality and to add a little sparkle to a dimly lit space. The colour chosen for the joinery contrasts with the red and gives it prominence. Set against red, the black lamps – their form emphasized by gilded lines – convince us that the red walls are lighter than they really are.

Our response to colour is emotional and associative. Colours can inspire strong feelings, reminding us of a particular time or place. Many of our notions about colours can be traced to their associations with the natural world – the restful green of a meadow, the blue of the sky or of the sea – and paint manufacturers' colour names reflect this. Some colours have acquired decorating associations through time-honoured practices: blue, for example, was once thought to repel flies and became the standard colour to paint a kitchen.

In interior decoration, particular colours and combinations of colour may bring to mind certain periods, but assigning a particular palette to a historical period is never straightforward: people have always had individual preferences and there will, no doubt, have been rooms decorated in shades outside the expected range. Furthermore, since each generation recreates the past for itself, reinterpreting it anew, any discussion of colour in historical decoration is not only subjective but also rooted in the context of our own times.

It is often thought that in the past the colours used in interior decoration were dark and dull, from a sombre and restricted palette. There is an element of truth in this notion, but it is influenced by present experience: the colours we see still surviving in historic rooms in houses open to the public, and the colours of rooms represented in old paintings, showing them when new, have all too often faded, been discoloured by layers of darkened varnish or distorted by ill-informed and unsympathetic restoration. It is remarkable the extent to which regular repainting can change the colour of a room, even if each repaint is thought to be in the original shade. If we could see how the colours looked before the years took their toll, we might well be surprised by the intensity and brilliance of historical colour schemes.

A further factor affects our perception and use of colour: uniform, bright artificial light and large panes of clear window glass give a high level of illumination which we take for granted in the twentieth century. Particularly at night, colours would have looked very different in the eighteenth century and qualities other than colour – the effect of glitter, sheen and matt finishes, for example – would have played a more significant role.

A Widening Palette

In the past, colours were restricted by the availability of pigments. Today, we are accustomed to the fact that almost any shade we want can be achieved in paint, fabric or print, but certain pigments and dyes were unknown before the last century and others were so expensive and rare that only the very rich could afford them. Pure titanium white, for example, became available only in the 1920s; until then white had nothing of the 'cleanness' of modern whites. And for a long time pure blue could be obtained only from ultramarine, made by grinding the semi-precious stone lapis lazuli; it was extremely expensive and so hardly used in decorating. Other blues were, by our standards, dull, until the 1720s, when Prussian blue, the first synthetic pigment produced, became available.

Archaeological techniques of research into colour are improving all the time and it is now possible to be more accurate about the colours that were used historically. What were considered to be authentic 'Georgian' colours in the 1930s, for example, would not convince today's experts, who conduct exhaustive analyses of samples of old paint. However, there are some drawbacks to drawing conclusions from their evidence. There is no foolproof way of knowing whether or not a 'scrape' has revealed the final colour or the underpainting. The process of taking samples can also destroy fine glazes and flatting coats which would have modified the base coat in subtle and unpredictable ways. Scientific

RIGHT *Although not definitive, this plate shows something of the range of colours in use during the eighteenth and early nineteenth centuries.* Top row *Lead colour, here in a dark and light version, was commonly used throughout the eighteenth century. The three 'wood' colours were used, in various strengths, for panelling and joinery.* Second row *Colours often seen in interior decoration in the eighteenth century. Subtlety and brilliance could be gained by glazing these colours over white or paler versions.* Third row *In the second half of the eighteenth century, the range of pigments increased as did the demand for more adventurous mixes.* Fourth row *Three 'Etruscan' or 'Pompeiian' colours, based on Etruscan vases and wall paintings that were discovered towards the end of the eighteenth century. French grey and Parma violet were two of the greys that became fashionable in the early nineteenth century.* Fifth row *Five colours that were popular in the early nineteenth century: olive had always been fashionable; the other colours are frequently seen in ceramics and wallpapers of the period. There was a great vogue for yellow in the second decade of the nineteenth century.*

LEFT *Ageing whitewash is decorated with a spirited pattern in harmonious earthy colours in this detail from a Swedish wall painting. The calligraphic flourishes in black stand out against the surrounding softness, where a subtle green balances a soft red. The grey of the crown and column-base, set against the comparative purity of the other slightly ochre colours, becomes almost blue.*

Neoclassical architects such as Robert Adam (1728–92) and Karl Friedrich Schinkel (1781–1841) were influential in their innovative use of strong colours which they considered as part of their overall architectural schemes – an expressive use of colour that would have been unthinkable at the beginning of the eighteenth century. Precision and clarity are as much the hallmarks of Schinkel's work as his distinctive use of colour. In a suite of rooms at Schloss Charlottenhof in Potsdam, Germany, the decoration of the rooms contributes to the overall vista. In the foreground, a lot of soft pink is set against strong pea-green, the composition kept cool by the use of silver. As the enfilade *progresses the combinations become richer: blue offset by gold and, finally, a bold red bordered by green to pull the focus forward.*

analysis may reveal the presence of, say, ochre earth, but not its exact hue – the colour of ochre can vary enormously depending on where it comes from. But historical research should always be kept in perspective – while the value of the academic understanding of the colours used historically should not be underestimated or ignored, the most important thing, for practical and everyday use, is that we are happy with our chosen colours. It is, after all, quite possible that some of the colours that have been revealed by research were rejected by their creators as failures and fast painted out.

Until the Industrial Revolution, the everyday colours used in decorating were derived from earth pigments which were both affordable and easy to come by. Although surprisingly bright colours can be made from earth pigments, especially where any neighbouring whites are not 'brilliant white', the basic eighteenth-century palette relied on 'stone' colours for wall surfaces and 'wood' colours for woodwork. These were essentially neutral shades of drab, grey, buff and various browns, from greenish raw umber and terre verte to pink and reddish burnt earths. Stronger blues and pea greens seem – like clearer yellows – to date from the 1760s onward.

The association between material and colour was reflected in the names given to the colours used: 'oak-panelling colour' or 'wainscot' signified shades of brown often painted on panelling. Brighter and more expensive colours, derived from rare or exotic pigments, were reserved for the best rooms in the better households, rooms which proclaimed the status and importance of the family. The use of bright, rich colours was strongly linked with the importance attached to fabrics – such as red damask – and these colours were most often introduced in the fabrics used for furnishings.

There was a significant shift in the use of colour in European interior decoration towards the end of the eighteenth century. The unearthing of the Pompeiian and Etruscan antiquities, and the upper-class vogue for visiting the Italian ruins, inspired a fashion for new bright colours, such as Pompeiian red. The demand for more vivid, arresting colours coincided with technological advances in chemical colour production which expanded the house-painter's palette.

In the 1820s, a clear, bright and reliable yellow became available for the first time as a result of the manufacture of chrome yellow, and this also meant that a bright green could be achieved easily. Both colours were highly fashionable in Empire and Regency schemes where complementary colours were often used together to produce heightened contrasts – yellow trimmed with purple, red with green.

Up to the middle of the nineteenth century, colour, like other elements of design and decoration, followed a consistent line of development, with new ideas being absorbed as they came along. By this time, a tremendous number of new pigments had been invented and made commercially available and new aesthetic discoveries were made and new influences unearthed. This coincided with the rapid growth of the middle-class market, which, together with expanded production and distribution, meant that there was less uniformity of development than had previously been the case.

The new chemical or 'aniline' pigments and dyes rapidly superseded natural pigments. Produced in factories, they were available cheaply in great quantities for the new market. As London's Great Exhibition of 1851 showed, the public wanted to recreate a sense of the past – and this involved much reproduction and stylistic plundering.

The mid-Victorian palette was garish: crimson, Prussian blue, maroon, yellow and deep green jostled uncomfortably for attention in polychromatic schemes. New colours included mauve, invented in 1846 and all the rage mid-century, and magenta, available in the 1860s and named after the Battle of Magenta of 1859.

Reaction soon followed, in the 1870s, with the Aesthetes and the practitioners of the Arts and Crafts movement. James Abbott McNeill Whistler's shocking Peacock Room and Dante Gabriel Rossetti's use of dark green were examples in which innovation and the deliberate avoidance of convention or tradition were every bit as important as the colour. 'Greenery-yallery' became the colour symbolizing the Aesthetes, gently satirized by Gilbert and Sullivan in *Patience* for their sensitivities. William Morris (1834–96) conducted extensive experiments in dyeing with natural or vegetable dyes, reviving a craft which had virtually disappeared over the course of a few decades and helping to sponsor a fashion for softer, more harmonious shades. The trend for lighter colours, even white, gained ground towards the end of the century.

In the twentieth century, there has been a wealth of options for colour in decorating. A fashion for intense 'jazz' colours – purple, orange, lime green and emerald – not unlike those of a century earlier, was specifically identified with Art Deco in the 1920s and '30s. But although every decade has had its own particular vogue colours, white has proved to be one of the most persistent choices.

The Modern movement in architecture and design set the standard for plain white walls during the early decades of the twentieth century; white was also popular in fashionable decorating circles of the 1920s and '30s, although the 'colour' as it was then used was very much subtler than the white to which we are accustomed today, and could be flat or shiny, applied as a glaze over red to show the faintest hint of pink, or softened with an ochre and umber glaze to become ivory. Each technique was used deliberately and thoughtfully – never in the spirit of 'two coats of white latex', with which we are now familiar.

Other colours were also used during this period with great skill and subtlety, almost akin to Adam's architectural application of colour. But, due to the combination of market forces and the disruptions of the Second World War, the tradition was broken until the recent widespread revival of interest in colour effects and a gradual return of confidence and a desire to experiment.

In an all-white scheme, the introduction of the merest hint of colour is eyecatching. In this room designed by Charles Rennie Mackintosh, the colours of the stencilled decoration have been deliberately suppressed and cooled with white so that, while they stand out, they do not do so at the expense of the unity of the room.

Choosing Colour

Faced with the bewildering variety of shades that are presented on a manufacturer's colour card, most people find it difficult to choose a colour. Many give up altogether and opt for something safe, a tried and tested formula, perhaps white or near-white. Or they may, having settled on a particular shade, wonder why it looks so bright, and so wrong, once on the wall.

Colour cannot be chosen in isolation and should relate to the conditions existing in the room: to the quality of light, both natural and artificial, and to the other surfaces and finishes, as well as to the room's furniture and pictures that are displayed in it. Any colour can be made to look brighter or duller by varying its context. There is also the question of appropriateness, what the room is used for and at what time of day. Most of us also have some idea of the type of colours we like best, our personal preferences – cool and light, dark and rich, or intense. We may feel drawn to a family of colours, to blues, greens or reds. If one is drawn to a colour, there is every reason to use it in decoration: there is no need to be hesitant and restrict oneself to neutral, serviceable backgrounds.

Armed with some knowledge, one is more likely to make a successful choice from a colour card or bundle of swatches. But it is important to be aware of the limitations of colour cards and manufacturers' catalogues. Most colour cards present a misleading picture. Colours are typically arranged in tiny squares, close to each other, in rows graduating from light to dark. Each square of colour is too small to enable one to make anything like an accurate assessment of the shade, especially as the surrounding paper is usually bright white. Further, the breadth of choice itself creates problems since few people will ever use the darkest or most intense colours on the cards for decorating – they are there largely for the sake of completeness. And because the colours are arranged in tones from light to dark, comparisons of relative brightness are difficult, making it easy to end up with a more intense shade than expected. Moreover, some colours – blue especially – 'mount up' and intensify in use, so that a barely blue grey-white on the colour card will become a distinctly blue room.

Catalogues, with their immaculate studio and location shots, present different pitfalls. Here, it is difficult to assess the actual appearance of the colour represented because what you are seeing is subject to the vagaries of the printing process and the effect of different types of lighting.

Manufacturers' sample pots, which enable small quantities of the colour to be tried out, are an obvious solution to the problem. There is really no substitute for experiment: painting a section of a wall is the best way of assessing a particular colour, its effect on its surroundings and how it looks under the room's light conditions. In the same way, a sample roll of wallpaper pinned up or a generous swatch of fabric draped over the piece intended for upholstery will give a far better picture than any colour card or swatch book.

Accepted decorating wisdom suggests that it is best to paint or decorate a dark room, which receives little natural daylight, in a light colour such as a pastel or neutral. In practice, this is often unsuccessful.

LEFT *Cool, even light filtered through the frosted panes of a skylight set flush with the ceiling, throws the warm tones of an old Dutch armoire into prominence. I first used this green wallcolour with a warm beige for the joinery – the result was that the beige looked pink. But here the slightly darker green, used in an eggshell finish, gives the wallcolour an attractive dryness. The 'wetting' effect of the eggshell finish on the joinery increases the tonal contrast between the two colours, and both appear lighter when compared with the dark bulk of the marquetry armoire.*

Seen in isolation as paint samples (ABOVE)*, the colours seem relatively dull, characterless and dark. Once applied, however, they are quite rich and the fact that the ceiling is in shadow makes them seem lighter.*

If there is not much natural light, subtle colours lose their subtlety and can even appear dingy and dirty. Strong, dark colours, on the other hand, have an innate richness and intensity which helps to counteract the lack of light. Likewise, a small room painted in a pale colour will, by revealing itself completely and immediately, hold no mysteries, leave no room for discovery. A dark colour can, by concealment and confusion, allow the small room to acquire hidden depths, to seem larger. Conversely, in a room which benefits from a lot of natural light, delicate, subtle colours can be fully appreciated and can help to spread the brightness around. The subtle colour schemes of the early nineteenth century, often relying on complementaries, were designed for rooms with big windows, bathed in natural light.

LEFT *A well-lit kitchen – its ceiling (beams, joists and all) thickly distempered in white – contrasts with a darker dining room. When first painted, the wallcolour was the same in both rooms, but to heighten contrast and to reduce the emphatic rhythm of the dark wood, I glazed the dining-room walls with a stronger red. Beamed ceilings like these were traditionally whitewashed or distempered – giving a sculptural effect quite different from the more usual black and white treatment that 'lowers' the ceiling.*

ABOVE *Many colours when used in strong mixes look better varnished. The reflections and surface glitter this produces, as seen in this drawing room, add interest and break up an area that might otherwise be heavy and solid. The complex play of light and shade, full of strong contrasts, ensures that the yellow does not prove overwhelming.*

The texture and gloss or flatness of the finish also affect the colour. Dark colours tend to look better in gloss or in finishes with a slight sheen. The highlights created by a reflective surface prevent the colour from looking dead. Great play was made of these contrasts in the nineteenth century, with shiny varnished paper contrasting with flock to enhance the textural variety. Similarly, these contrasts were enjoyed in the 1920s. The designer Basil Ionides (1884–1950), for instance, would use gloss paint sparingly as a way of picking out mouldings and would exploit the differences between distemper and whitewash, flat oil paint and gloss.

COMBINING COLOURS

When it comes to combining colours in a decorative scheme, many people are especially hesitant. They may well be able to choose one colour with confidence but find it difficult to decide which other colours would go with it. The art of combining colours is largely a matter of proportion; in practice this means that, for example, you can put a small amount of brilliant colour with a duller shade, as a trimming or accent, but equal amounts of two bright colours will not 'settle down'. The same principle applies if you are combining several colours: the proportion of the main colour to the subsidiary shades is critical and it is often a good idea if the main colour harmonizes with one of the lesser colours – colours that 'harmonize' lie close to each other on the colour wheel and their harmony is the result of shared ingredients. Alternatively, if one is setting up a vibrant relationship between two colours, there should be an intermediate and mitigating quiet shade to provide visual respite. Yellow walls, for example, with vibrant blue edging, could be combined effectively with white or perhaps black doors or a plain, neutral carpet. With multicoloured schemes, one shade should be allowed to predominate and any clashes – often a feature of such schemes – should be kept small-scale so as to allow the main theme to be clearly heard.

In combining colours, as in many other aspects of decoration, observation is important. Inspiration can be drawn not only from successful colour schemes seen in books and magazines but also from

RIGHT *The colour of the walls above the dado in this sitting room has great strength and, while not cold, is cool and undemanding. The balanced quantities of blue and red in the carpet and sofa sit happily together and the overall scheme is unified by the use of neutral off-whites.*

LEFT *Sir John Soane's use of colour is as distinctive as his architecture. The strong red, a 'Pompeiian' colour, is combined with a green that is at one and the same time the complementary colour and a reminder of the colour of old bronze. This detail is from the library, a 'through' room, which although lit from both ends does not receive much light. The use of vibrant complementary colours is a way of enlivening surfaces that might otherwise seem dull.*

gardens, shops, fabric patterns and paintings. Examples of good colour combinations are to be found everywhere. One should train oneself to enquire what it is that makes them work, to determine which are the neutral areas, what the dominant colour is and where and in what proportion its complementary is used. Complementaries are those colours which lie opposite each other on the colour wheel: green is opposite to red, purple opposite to yellow, and so on. The reason why such complementary colours 'work' together is to do with the mechanism of the eye itself. In practice what happens is that such opposites spark each other off.

COLOUR MIXING

Despite the wide range of shades of ready-mixed paints that are commercially available today, you can achieve a greater degree of subtlety and more variety by mixing your own colours, a process which is ultimately very rewarding. All paints, at their simplest, are made of colour usually in the form of both powder, which has bulk, and stainer, which has no bulk; of a medium (the glue that dries and sticks the colour to the wall); and of a vehicle (the oil, water or spirit that makes the mixture brushable). Paints are either oil-based or water-based. Oil-based paints can vary between the shiny gloss or 'enamel', and non-shiny flat finishes. Water-based paints are mostly flat, although some latex paints are available in a mid-sheen.

In colour mixing, it is the mixing of hues which is significant, while the type of paint – whether it is oil- or water-based – is irrelevant. Nevertheless, in practice, it is vital to differentiate between the two. Water-based paints can be tinted only with water-soluble substances – which are usually thinned first with water to make mixing easier. The substances used are latex paint, gouache, tempera, poster paint or watercolour, ink, food dye, universal stainers, acrylics or pigments (dry powders) mixed with water. Oil-based paints can be tinted only with other oil paint (artists' oils will need to be diluted in turpentine first), with universal stainers or with pigments ground in turpentine or oil. Adding pigments or universal stainers to a paint will reduce its strength and adding too much can produce an unstable mix that would never dry or, if it did, would then crumble very fast. Colour mixing is something of an art and requires practice and a good eye. The basic method, however, is straightforward.

The first step is to choose a base colour, which should be paler than the 'goal' colour. If the colour you intend to mix is light, it is usually best to start from white and tint it. More intense colours, however, cannot be based on white and for these you need to select the nearest shade you can find from a commercial range.

To experiment, to feel your way into a colour, put a little of the base colour onto a palette, plate or sheet of glass. Then gradually, with a small brush, add different pigments, to find which ones take the colour in the direction you want. Once you are getting near the right shade, paint a sample onto a scrap of lining paper or a postcard and allow it to dry. You can 'force dry' with a hairdryer, but beware of drying it too fast – the colour can be distorted by heat. Oil paint tends to dry darker than it

This sample shows how different paint mediums change colour in different ways as they dry. When mixing colours this must be taken into account. Only dry samples should be used for colour matching. From top to bottom:

This sample is in distemper. The colour at the left, darker and more intense, is freshly painted. As the paint dries, the white seems to rise to the surface.

In latex the same effect is observed, though it is less marked.

In oil paint (eggshell here), the colour darkens and intensifies as it dries.

If one needs two very close tones of the same colour, in oil say, it can be useful to match a wet sample to a dry sample. When dry, the newly mixed paint will be one step darker than the dry sample to which it was matched.

appears when wet. In order to be able to recreate the exact colour, keep a record of the approximate proportions of the different pigments you use in relation to the base colour. When you are satisfied with the results, you can then go on to mix the shade in bulk.

The process of colour mixing is helped considerably by some understanding of colour relationships. If you add a colour to its opposite you reduce its intensity: if, for example, you are mixing a dull, pale yellow you would start by adding yellow – whether warm or sharp – to white until you have got somewhere near the desired shade, and would then dull it by adding its complementary, in this case purple, in small quantities. It is easy to mix colours that harmonize: yellow added to green will take the green one way, blue in the opposite direction.

It is unusual to find a ready-made paint colour to match a fabric and you may have to mix your own to achieve the exact shade. However, which shade should you choose to match? In this bathroom, the salmon-coloured walls match the pattern rather than the background colour of the toile de Jouy fabric.

Choosing and mixing colours

It is often a good idea to choose paint colours for a room by looking at fabric swatches. The changing light on a piece of material means that the colour can be 'read' with more flexibility than would be possible with a paint sample. The fabric you choose can serve as an effective colour-matching guide when mixing colours for painting.

This fabric is printed with an eighteenth-century design. The colours are muted and balanced. The red background colour is softened visually by the use of a stronger red in the detail.

To mix a red for walls or any surface, using fabric as a colour guide, start with a ready-made paint that is close to the colour you require. It is easier to start with a colour that is paler than the goal colour and darken it, rather than the other way round.

The red (rows 1 and 2, from left to right)

1 Crimson is squeezed straight from the tube. This colour is too intense.

2 Adding white makes a pink that is nearer in tone to the fabric but reveals the blueness present in crimson.

3 To counteract the blue, add a warm yellow. Yellow ochre turns the paint slightly orange. This is now getting near the goal colour but is too bright.

4 To cool it down and to reduce the redness, mix in raw umber which is a greeny brown (green being the complementary of red). The colour is now very close and a little juggling with the colours will produce the desired effect.

To make large quantities of colour based on this information, choose a ready-made red and, in the light of experience gained in the tests, adjust it to match until you are happy with the result. Make a note of the approximate proportions of the colours used in the experiment so that you are able to achieve the same colour in bulk.

The white (rows 3 and 4, from left to right)

1 The first trial is of white with a little black. This is clearly too cold.

2 Adding a warm brown – a burnt umber – makes a colour that is of the wrong hue and that is going in completely the wrong direction.

3 Starting from scratch again, white and raw umber are mixed together. This is the right approach, but a little extra 'life' is still needed.

4 Adding yellow ochre makes a dramatic difference and the goal colour is achieved.

Making large quantities of colours based on white is quite easy. The process is the same as described above except that a bucket of white and cupfuls of colour are used rather than a few brushfuls. Try out small quantities first to fix the recipe. Then make the large quantity. Add the colour gradually. Tube colours will need diluting first to help them mix (oil colours should be diluted with turpentine, acrylic colours with water).

The nineteenth century had high standards for preparing and decorating surfaces, The Paper-Hanger, Painter, Grainer and Decorator's Assistant *(1879) recommending a minimum of six stages for new woodwork. Few people are as rigorous today. The same procedure has been applied to this sample (from left to right): sandpaper the surface and seal the knots with shellac knotting; apply primer and stop up any nail-holes and cracks with putty; apply an undercoat and rub down; apply a top coat and rub down; apply a second top coat and rub down lightly; apply a flatting coat (here it is slightly paler than the second top coat).*

In addition to the above, the manual recommends that the surface should be cleaned frequently with a dusting brush and a tack rag should be used immediately before each coat is applied.

HOW TO PAINT

Before you begin to paint, you must ensure that the surface is sound and well-prepared. In the case of walls, this means stripping off old paper or lining paper, filling cracks and holes, making sure that the plaster is dry and not greasy, crumbly or flaky. Historically, new plasterwork was treated with size or linseed oil to seal it; sealing made paint easier to apply and stopped it from being drawn into the wall and weakening the finish. Nowadays proprietary primers are available for sealing plaster; an alternative is to use thinned shellac, which is cheaper and has the additional advantage of not leaving brushmarks.

After the preparatory work, apply an undercoat, followed by one or two top coats. The number of coats should depend on the finish that is required rather than on the manufacturers' instructions: if you don't like the effect after one coat, apply another. Each coat should be allowed to dry before the next is applied. The amount of time this takes will vary but follow the guidelines that are given. If you use the paint fairly thinly you will find it quick-drying, economical and versatile. Manufacturers' recommendations understandably err on the side of caution, but paint is something that can be applied quickly, particularly if the surface has been prepared and undercoated well.

Using a roller for painting results in a horrible mechanical finish. It is far better to use a brush: choose a size scaled to your hand and strength and work consistently, from top to bottom and, if right-handed, from right to left. A 10cm/4in brush covers twice as much wall as a 5cm/2in brush. Don't be afraid to thin the paint to make the job easier – thin coats of paint can be brushed on quickly and easily.

Despite obvious variations, the basic sequence is the same for painting woodwork as it is for painting walls (the sample below follows the guidelines that are set out in a nineteenth-century decorator's manual). Again, it is worth taking the trouble to prepare and paint the surface properly – too few coats of paint and not enough rubbing down will inevitably result in an impoverished and unsatisfactory finish. An extra coat of paint in the early stages, rubbed down thoroughly and then wiped with a tack rag, will be well worthwhile.

Broken Colour

The enormous popularity of broken colour work over the last decade or so has not always produced happy results. The art of broken colour is so seductive that the temptation has been to overdo it, in terms of both colour and pattern. In some interiors, everything is ragrolled, a fascination with technique at the expense of effect. Success with broken colour work demands the opposite approach: the techniques you decide to use (and you may need to adopt several) are to be seen as the means of achieving a particular effect or colour, and not an end in themselves.

Broken colour work and the use of glazes often take advantage of the transparent medium, the scumble glaze, which retains the marks created in applying it. The colours produced are not solid since the glaze allows light to pass back and forth through the now translucent colour to the undercoat.

It is important to begin with an idea of the colour or texture you wish to reproduce and then to experiment with various methods until you

This luminous pink was created by dragging one coat of a dark crimson glaze twice – first horizontally, then, when dry, vertically – over white eggshell. This colour would be impossible to achieve in a solid paint without it being too dark or too 'sugary'.

achieve the result you want. For many broken colour methods that involve working or 'distressing' a top coat while it is still wet, oil glaze is generally the best medium because the slower drying time allows greater flexibility. But there are situations when washes of water-based paint can be very effective, and cases where the unique dryness of casein is all-important.

Broken colour generally works best when used subtly, either by reducing the contrast between base coat and top coat or, if there is to be a strong contrast between the two shades, by ensuring that the pattern of, for example, the brushstrokes of the broken coat is less insistent. Ragrolling, the most strident of the broken colour techniques, can be particularly effective when two shades that are close in tone are used – pale cream over white, for example, can suggest the subtlety of a self-patterned fabric such as damask. These basic principles were well appreciated in fashionable decorating circles in the 1920s and '30s, when to achieve a subtle grey that was not dead might have involved grey or even two greys being stippled over a blue background and worked with the finest hair stippler, until almost every trace of blue – but not quite all – had been obliterated.

RIGHT In this mid-eighteenth-century room, bold mouldings articulate the walls. The joinery is painted in a flat-oil paint glaze; the dado panel is slightly darker than the mouldings and the baseboard is black. The whites have a touch of yellow in them to enhance the blue of the walls.

The walls were first distempered in pale grey. The same distemper was then turned blue by the addition of blue universal stainer, added little by little until the distemper acquired a definite blueness (but no further). Once thinned out with water, the mixture was brushed onto the walls and then immediately stippled with a hair stippler. This job requires two people – one brushing, the other stippling – as speed is essential. The result is a minutely flecked texture, with the blue kept 'quiet' by the tiny pocks of grey.

LEFT These samples show the effect of a strong colour contrast applied with a subtle technique, and a subtle colour contrast using a strong technique.

In the first sample, a bright blue has been dragged over off-white. The fairly strong contrast between the coats is tempered by the fine texture of the dragging.

The second sample shows sponging in pink on pink. The potential roughness of the finish is reduced because the two coats are quite close in tone. Had there been still less difference between them, the pattern could have been more uneven without destroying the integrity of the finish.

ABOVE *This sample, worked in four stages, is based on an early-nineteenth-century colour scheme and demonstrates how an undercoat can affect the final colour. The pink base coat influences the acid yellow top coats and together they produce an intense and balanced colour, with 'life' introduced in the slightly uneven texture of the brushstrokes. Each coat was allowed to dry before the next was applied.*

The background was painted a strong fuchsia pink eggshell. Then a paint glaze was made up using a little white (for opacity) and a cold yellow (cadmium yellow, light), extended in scumble glaze and thinned with turpentine. Three coats of the glaze (allowed to dry between each application) were needed to produce the final colour.

RIGHT *Here, yellow colourwashed walls are offset by weathered green shutters. The timelessness of this finish is one of its advantages and the fact that it can sustain some wear, without looking as though it needs repainting, will recommend it to many.*

USING GLAZES

A glaze can be a coat of paint of any kind, thinned to translucency with turpentine or mineral spirit for oil-based paints or with water for water-based paints. Oil glazes can be made using a mixture of scumble glaze, pigments or stainers and turpentine or white spirit. Scumble glaze is a proprietary product, akin to 'megilp', the medium which artists add to their oil paint to make transparent glazes. Scumble glaze does not run but remains workable for some time. Like varnish, it is colourless; unlike varnish, it retains – even when thinned out to a watery consistency – any brushstroke that is left in it. The pigments or stainers add colour to the glaze; the turpentine or mineral spirit makes the mixture brushable. Flat oil paint can also be added to give a matt finish or (in white) if white is needed in the colour. Indeed, all the pale off-white glazes will have nearly as much white flat oil as scumble glaze.

Glazes are used (as opposed to opaque paints) as top coats in broken colour methods to give subtlety and depth. They may be applied unevenly so that patches of the background colour show through or they may be distressed while still wet, so that patches of the glaze are lifted off to reveal the base coat. A glaze can also be the means of rescuing a colour which does not look right, adjusting its tone or intensity. Coloured glazes applied over white or over a pale undercoat always seem to turn out brighter than they looked in the pot; and mixed colours, when used as a glaze, can seem to separate into their constituent parts – blue, for example, tends to re-emerge from mixtures.

USING WASHES AS GLAZES

Broken colour work using distemper or emulsion is a different process from oil-glazing. These water-based paints dry very much more quickly than oil, which means there is no time for subtle working. Washes – made by thinning the paint with water – have to be brushed on directly and immediately. The effect relies on the evenness and rhythm of the brushmarks for its inherent liveliness.

Thinned distemper used over a distempered background will not run. Due to the high absorbency of distemper, the brushmarks will be 'seized' immediately. Latex, however, is harder to handle. Experiment will reveal the right degree of thinning – the wash should be thin but should not run. Latex glazes can be made using an acrylic varnish, rather than water, to thin the paint and make it more like an oil glaze. This is similar to the eighteenth-century use of paste as a medium for printing decorated papers with translucent colour.

BROKEN COLOUR METHODS

The following techniques are the most common of the broken colour methods and, in general, the results will be more subtle if used in a subtractive rather than an additive method: lifting colour off while it is still wet is generally less brash than applying it as a 'print'. But working in a subtractive way can be a race against time. It is often best to apply the top coat in sections, about 60cm/2ft wide, which can be comfortably worked without the surface drying out and, in particular, without the edges drying.

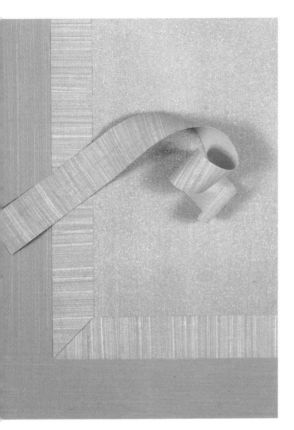

Broken colour work can be difficult to handle in the corners of rooms and along edges and baseboards. One solution to the problem is to stick borders on top of the paintwork to produce a neat finish, in much the same manner as a braid or fillet is used in wallpapered or upholstered rooms. Such borders can be made by dragging on prepared lining paper, as here.

Some methods, such as sponging, are specifically associated with the pattern made by a certain tool or material. For others, a particular type of brush may be required and its size and the texture of its bristles will determine the final result. In most cases, whatever method or tool is chosen, it is the edges of the walls which prove to be the most difficult parts to get right. Either the paint tends to build up towards the edge, giving a clogged look, or it fades away revealing too much of the undercoat. Fading the pattern out into the corner is a tricky process; it may be easier to go round afterwards with a dry brush and take the glaze out of the corner. In some situations it may be possible to mask out the edges with strips of tape, to paint over the tape and then to remove it leaving a crisp edge. But the easiest way is to avoid the problem altogether and cover up the edges with borders, made from wallpaper, gimp, braid or fabric.

To make a virtually invisible neat edge, you could make matching painted borders using lining paper. Paint the paper with the same preparatory coats as the wall and then drag it with the same colour as that used on the walls. When the paper is dry, cut it into strips about 2.5cm/1in wide and paste these around the edges of the room. This treatment neatens the walls in the same way as woven tape binding neatens the edges of fabric.

Alternatively, go for contrast. Make a feature out of the edges by painting them in any technique with a contrasting colour, chosen to accentuate the main shade, intensifying or brightening it.

When using broken colour techniques, the walls can be finished off by varnishing with gloss, eggshell or flat. Any varnish will alter the appearance of the walls and oil varnishes tend to yellow with age (as will the glaze medium in those places where it is deprived of light). Water-based varnishes are generally not as strong as oil-based varnishes but the colour varies less. A matt water-based varnish is usually the best choice, except in bathrooms, where oil-based varnish should be used in order to protect the walls or surfaces from steam. The most suitable oil-based varnishes will have a slight purple tinge to them which successfully counteracts the yellowing effect.

STIPPLING

Stippling results in a mottled, even finish which is often very effective if top and base coats are quite different in tone or colour from one another. Stippling was originally intended as a remedial technique to remove all trace of brushmarks.

Stippling is hard work. The method involves brushing on a top coat of glaze and then, using even pressure, going over the wet coat, lifting off minute patches of colour. You can use either a stippling brush which has long soft hairs, very closely packed, a rag stippler or a rubber stippler, which gives a coarser effect. The need to apply the same degree of pressure all over the wall is what makes the technique so tiring. There will be at least 200 strokes – where the brush is struck into the wet glaze – every minute. A large wall might take an hour and a half of unremitting brushing on and stippling – the only respite is in those brief moments when the ladder has to be moved.

These three samples show the different effects produced from a hair stippler, a rubber stippler and a rag stippler. In all examples, the glaze is brushed onto the wall in areas as large as can be managed and then stippled. It is the way in which the glaze is lifted off that produces the pattern. The glaze must be worked before it dries up and the joins blended between patches of work. The edges and corners of the wall are more difficult to stipple than the middle – consequently, less glaze is taken off in these areas. The stippler should be wiped clean from time to time.

The hair stippler is used to even out the coat of translucent glaze to produce an *almost* textureless finish (TOP). It is the subtlest way of using a glaze.

The rubber stippler is larger than the hair stippler and is also used for texturing plaster (MIDDLE). By constantly changing the angle of the stippler, the glaze can be broken into a close, even pattern which can be rather insistent.

With rag stippling (BOTTOM), a soft crumpled rag is used to break up the glaze in a random pattern to produce an attractive, clouded finish.

RAGGING AND RAGROLLING

Ragging and ragrolling as subtractive techniques involve the use of a cloth or rag to lift off wet glaze. In ragging, the surface is dabbed with the cloth; in ragrolling, a crumpled sausage of cloth is rolled down over the surface to produce a pattern with a greater sense of movement and flow. Ragging is part of the repertoire of methods involved in marbling, where it is used to break up a ground colour or glaze before adding veins or taking them out with turpentine.

The type of 'print' that you achieve will depend to a large extent on the type of cloth you use. Good absorbent cloths include heavy muslin and worn-out cotton sheets. If you choose something with a more obvious texture, such as a cloth with tiny square holes, the 'print' will be that much more emphatic. Chamois leather leaves a pattern which resembles crushed velvet; crumpled paper gives a sharp, hard-edged 'print'. Avoid using newspaper – the print comes off!

Another factor affecting the quality of the pattern is how often the rag is changed. If you persevere with the same rag, you will eventually reach the point where it is paint-sodden and you will be adding paint where the surface is thin and taking it off where the surface is thick. This will produce a clouded, mottled finish which can be very attractive. For a crisper effect, change the rag for a fresh one as soon as it is saturated.

To avoid a brash look, it is important to keep the top coat and base colour close in tone. The finish will also be more restrained if you keep going with the rag, moving it around in your hand and bunching it in different ways.

Ragging is akin to stippling, but the object is to leave a much larger pattern. In ragrolling (shown here), the pattern made by rolling a clean, crumpled cloth through the glaze is allowed to remain as the finish. More subtly, the shape of the rag can be constantly changed to create a 'marbled' effect.

In this example, the rag has been turned, rolled and reshaped and attention has been paid to taking out any large areas of untouched glaze.

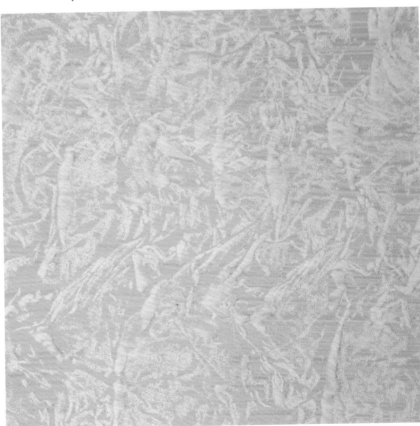

SPONGING

Sponging is the method originally adopted by the nineteenth-century painter-decorator to simulate granite and was used as an alternative to the rather more genteel technique of spattering. It involves using a sponge to dab on the top coat, with the grain of the sponge – a natural, marine sponge – giving the characteristic print. The effect can be bold or subdued depending on the colours used, the density of the patterning and the texture of the sponge. Usually executed in watercolour, sponging can be done in oil paint or glaze, but this is more difficult. Before being dipped in the glaze the sponge must be wetted to soften it – not with mineral spirit which would dilute the glaze, but with water.

A fine example of sponging in which, in the first sample, a warm darkish cream disappears in stages beneath blue and off-white. Mask out corners and edges before sponging. Allow each step to dry thoroughly.

1 Paint the surface with a warm cream latex.

2 Thin out a blue (made from phthalocyanine blue and white latex) with water to the consistency of single cream. Wet a marine sponge, squeeze it dry and dip into the blue, squeeze again and test on waste paper. Then press the sponge lightly to the surface, constantly changing direction and angle to build up an even cover. Work broadly – do not concentrate on small areas. Wash the sponge out thoroughly.

3 Use a second mix, this time white with a little yellow ochre, and apply in the same way. Wash out the sponge again.

4 Apply a third coat of sponging, as step 3 but with a little more white added. The more coats of sponging and the closer the colours, the subtler the effect.

Using the same technique to imitate lapis lazuli, sponge in layers as follows:

1 Sponge bright yellow on a white ground in irregular drifts.

2 and 3 Sponge ultramarine over until it becomes as dense as the colour shown in band 3.

4 Sponge on a Payne's grey and ultramarine mix to darken. Use a fine-grained sponge so that tiny pieces of ultramarine are visible.

5 Wash over the surface with waves and bands of ultramarine to heighten the colour or of Payne's grey to darken some areas – this will even out the spottiness.

DRAGGING

Dragging, when used on walls rather than on woodwork, produces a finish which can resemble a woven material. It can be a good way of emphasizing the vertical, visually extending the height of a room. The basic tool is either a dragging brush or the same wide brush used for applying the glaze. The oil-glaze is applied and the brush used to drag down through the wet finish, removing paint in fine parallel lines. The coarseness or fineness of the brush will influence the quality of the finish. Because it is impossible to drag the whole wall from top to bottom in a single stroke, it must be done in two movements – down from the top as far as possible and then up from the bottom keeping the pattern even and the lines straight. The height of the join where the two strokes meet must be staggered along the length of the wall or there will be an obvious horizontal seam.

Crossdragging is an extension of the technique. After the wall has been dragged vertically and when it is quite dry – say a day later – it is dragged horizontally: the result is an even better simulation of fabric. This type of finish can also be effective on a small scale, such as for the interior of a box or display case – unlike fabric lining, a dragged finish can be washed and will not discolour, especially if it is varnished.

The technique of dragging (TOP) is not difficult but making neat tops and bottoms to each stroke is. The glaze must be thin enough to lift easily.

For dragging, brush bands of glaze about 60cm/2ft wide onto the wall and drag through, either with the same brush used for the glaze or with one reserved for the job. Take care to effect neat joins between bands.

Crossdragging (BOTTOM) is simply dragging twice. Drag once, vertically, and then apply another coat of glaze and, when dry, drag again horizontally. The glaze should be thinner than that used for ordinary dragging so that the lines are more open.

SPATTERING

Spattering is a technique in which flecks of paint are knocked off the end of a brush onto a surface to produce a fine, regular speckled effect. By spattering with dots of colour a surface is given texture and pattern and its overall colour is also changed: a yellow wall, for example, could be flecked with a fine blue spatter to produce a gently muted green finish. To be successful, the work should be even and the spots small and of equal size. Spattering can be done on any surface, but it is messy and requires careful masking out of areas not being worked on. The process is simple but practise on newspaper first. The more paint there is left on the brush the bigger the spots will be and and the more they will be concentrated in lines that follow the direction of the brush. In addition, curved surfaces will take the spatters unevenly. The technique can be carried out in any kind of paint, on any kind of background. The thinner the paint, or glaze, the smaller the dots.

The technique can also be used to simulate porphyry. In Neoclassical schemes, the luxurious material was often simulated, usually as a trimming of some kind, perhaps on an architrave, a mantelpiece or an urn. To simulate porphyry, a background of purplish red is successively spattered with off-white, dark grey or black and finally, off-white again, to build up the characteristic speckled surface. Real porphyry will have some larger 'rogue' spots and even the occasional tiny grey wiggly vein. These can be added at random but with discretion, as they represent defects.

This sample (worked, from left to right, in bands) shows two 'spatters' on top of a plain colour.

Load a brush with paint, and squeeze dry on the side of the paint bucket and then spin (in the kettle above the paint) between the palms of the hands so that the excess paint, which must be fairly wet, travels down the bristles. Then tap against a stick at a distance of 30cm/12in or so from the work. The paint is spattered onto the surface in flecks or spots (depending on quantity and wetness). It is important to work over a broad area rather than concentrate on one spot.

By varying the colour of each layer of spattering the colour of the finished work can be altered.

THE
STONY
ROOM

Cool and dry, sculptural and monochromatic, the Stony Room has long been part of our decorative vocabulary. It may be in a plain, 'stony' colour, or it may subtly suggest, in its surface decoration, the distinctive textural properties of stone. Elaborate illusionist techniques may express the richness of classical stonework or, in a more romantic vein, the mellowed, crumbling stone of ancient ruins.

Stone colours have a subtlety and a sense of strength and solidity that is appropriate and expected in corridors or passages, on stairs and landings. Their neutral quality is valuable in areas which connect rooms, providing an easy visual transition between different schemes of decoration. For such areas, which are often used as places of display, perhaps for collections of pictures, prints or sculpture, a neutral background is ideal. Stone colours can also be used to accentuate more intensely coloured areas, showing them off to advantage; when combined with even small amounts of brilliant colour, the effect is rich and luminous. In pale versions, stony colours suit well-lit spaces, areas that benefit from natural light and where the subtleties of surface and tint can be appreciated.

The Stony Palette

Natural colours derived from stone and earth – whites, browns and greys and the dull greens, yellows and reds – these make up the stony palette. Subdued and comparatively dull, without being dark, their effect in monochromatic schemes is to focus attention on the quality of the wall surface itself. Indeed, in successful stony rooms it is hard to separate colour from texture. In a white room, of whatever shade, however warm or cool, dark or light, the quality of the finish is more evident than if the wall were intensely coloured or patterned. Slight irregularities of the surface mean that the light is picked up and reflected unevenly. This regular unevenness can be suggested or simulated on an over-smooth surface by the subtle use of broken colour.

When assembling any colour scheme, whether it comprises 'stone' colours or more intense shades, a basic rule of thumb is that warm colours make cool colours look cooler and vice versa. The final effect

The qualities and colours of stone can be rendered in paint in a variety of ways and the effect may be cool, and slightly austere, or romantic, capturing something of the quality of ancient ruins, crumbling with age. Light and shadow lend further drama to these somewhat theatrical interiors.

In this converted sixteenth-century Italian coastal watchtower, the designer Renzo Mongiardino has introduced a romantic vision of antiquity, inspired by J.L. Clérisseau's 1760's Scheme for a Ruin Room in Rome (see page 50). Real stone and trompe l'oeil effects have been combined in a masterly way, with the rough plaster reinforcing the illusion. Tonal balance between the painted highlights and shadows is nicely judged so as not to disturb the real chiaroscuro caused by the natural light falling from the opening to the roof terrace at the top of the spiral stairs.

LEFT *Experiment soon shows how to mix colours for the stony palette. Across the top are the pigments most frequently used: black, raw umber, burnt umber, yellow ochre, raw sienna, burnt sienna and Venetian red. Beneath these is a row of strong tints made from these pigments mixed with white. The third, fourth and fifth rows show some of the huge and subtle variety of colours that can result from the mixing of these pigments. Broadly speaking the colours in the sample relate directly to the pigments at the top, but those on the left are tempered by the addition of raw umber and those on the right are brightened by adding yellow ochre.*

At the bottom are four rectangles of a 'balanced' off-white – raw umber, yellow ochre and a little black mixed with increasing amounts of white. The long strip at the bottom is the palest of this series, which being 'neutral' – neither particularly warm nor cold – will sit happily between colours and tints that are both warmer and cooler.

RIGHT *Natural materials are combined to create a 'stony' effect in a Cambridgeshire manor house whose ancient timbers, markedly cool and silvery, are shown off to advantage by the dry pink limewash used on the plaster. The thick, plastery lime blends sympathetically with the pale grainy oak.*

depends on the proportions of the colours. A warm grey wall (grey with a pink or brown tinge) makes cool grey mouldings look bluer and colder. For a uniform effect, all the colours should share the same degree of warmth or coolness. In stony rooms, the play between warm and cool is one of the subtleties that is most to be enjoyed.

Simple Stone Finishes

For real depth of colour, good texture and finish and the ability to age well – even beautifully – it is important to use the kind of paint that will best express the surface qualities. Although stone colours can be found, more or less, in commercial paint ranges, they seldom match, either in colour or in finish, the classic decorator's paint, flat oil, which, although it is an oil paint, has no shine. This long-lasting paint is available in a range of colours as well as in black and white – white is used as a base for tinting with artists' oil colours or universal stainers. Earth pigments, including raw and burnt umber, raw and burnt sienna, yellow ochre, Naples yellow and red ochre, are used to mix the stone colours. 'Burnt' pigments, which have been subjected to red heat, are hotter colours than their raw counterparts. (The process of colour mixing is covered in greater detail on pages 24–7.)

DISTEMPER

With its chalky finish, distemper perfectly simulates the effect of stone, or of an old stone wall with layers of paint built up on it over the years. Oil-bound distemper was the chief household paint for walls and ceilings until the emergence of latex paint after the Second World War; wholly synthetic and easy to use, latex found a ready market among home decorators and improvers, though it has never found such favour with professionals, for whom real paint will be flat oil or, for its inimitable flatness and dryness, distemper.

After virtually disappearing for a generation, distemper has recently made a welcome comeback and is now available in several colours, including a good range of stony colours. Stronger colours, those not based on white pigment, can be specially made up or mixed at home using pigments and other ingredients available from a trade supplier. A wall which has already been painted should be prepared with a matt latex or flat oil as a key for distemper and, since distemper is incompatible with stronger modern finishes, it must be completely removed – or, as a poor second best, stabilized with a proprietary stabilizer – before returning to standard paints.

There are three main types of distemper. The first is whitewash or 'soft' distemper, a very fragile but beautiful finish, coming off easily to the touch, and composed of pigment, size and water. This is the kind of paint made and used by theatrical scene painters for generations. Quick and easy to produce with no more equipment than buckets and a gas ring, cheap and immensely versatile, it has a non-reflecting surface and a quick drying time. Its strength depends on the proportion of size in the recipe. Despite its name, whitewash can be tinted. It can be further strengthened by the addition of latex glaze.

Oil-bound distemper is a stronger form in which, again, the medium is water, but bound with a casein size and strengthened with linseed oil. Like soft distemper it is easy to apply and it can also be used thinned out as a glaze. On outside walls, the surface of oil-bound distemper gradually disintegrates and discolours in a charming way – unlike the more generally used exterior 'stone' paints which tend to peel entirely. Oil-bound distemper has the added advantage of allowing the wall to breathe, and thus does not trap moisture in the structure.

The third type of distemper is limewash, an often misused term. This is a specialist paint, which is tricky to use – it requires constant stirring, it cannot be applied to surfaces that are chemically incompatible with it, and it can only be tinted with pigments that do not discolour with lime. Its principal use is in situations where its weatherproofing qualities are important, as, for example, on the exterior and interior walls of churches. It hardens by means of a chemical reaction involving lime, rather in the nature of lime plaster – to which it is a close relation.

Creamy, limewashed walls are linked to a terracotta floor by the typically Italian device of painting a 'skirting' in a terracotta colour. This treatment makes a cool foil for the muted colours of the old tiles, wood and oriental kelims. The flimsy white bedhangings fill with light, reinforcing the dryness of the colours and textures in this Italian farmhouse.

Polished terracotta tiles are again linked to whitewashed walls by the painting of a 'skirting' in a strong terracotta colour (here the colours used were probably burnt umber and yellow ochre with a little white). Whitewash has also been used to colour the wood – either one thin coat, or a thicker coat painted on and rubbed off while still wet. This scheme ensures that the mellow colour of the ageing tiles shines out.

Coat upon coat of distemper can be applied to build up to a beautiful stony surface, especially on an uneven wall. Distemper used to create a broken finish gives an even more overtly stony effect. A traditional trick is to finish off with a pale coat, a shade lighter than the underlying layer. If this final coat is brushed on loosely and fast, with a sure hand, it will be slightly streaky, appearing to sit on top of the surface. The result gives a particularly convincing stony look: the translucent top layer imitates the dry chalky surface of stone and the thicker strokes in the uneven finish look like flecks of light in a way that suggests texture even on the smoothest of surfaces.

Just as stone ages and weathers, so these more natural paints also age beautifully. With time, the surface gently powders away and can even stain sympathetically. Latex paint, however, cannot behave in the same fashion and always betrays its origins. Even when sensitively painted, it will always remain a sheet of plastic. Its immutability can be a drawback if the natural, time-altered look is the goal.

SANDY TEXTURES

Another way of suggesting the texture of stone is to use sand to create a gritty finish. This method, which was used in the eighteenth century, is akin to the practice of applying gilding over sand, for example on parts of mirror or picture frames. The sand breaks up the surface reflections, giving a different colour to the glitter from that on the surrounding burnished gold. This treatment was used on some wooden exteriors of North American and English houses in the eighteenth century, where it was perhaps intended to prolong the life of the finish. Sand was peppered onto the last coat but one while it was still wet to produce the texture. The same technique can be used indoors, in appropriate stony colours (and, indeed, modern 'stone' paints incorporate just such a grainy texture in the mix).

Layering distemper
Coats of distemper build up to make an interesting surface. In this sample the final, fourth, coat is of almost pure white distemper (with a little raw umber added to take the edge off it) but the penultimate coat was considerably darker. The open quality of the top coat, and the rhythm of brushstrokes that results from working fast in a material that dries extremely quickly (almost as soon as it is applied), give a distinctive stony finish.

Sand in paint
This technique creates a real, physical texture. Sand is peppered onto wet paint (or glue) and the rough surface this creates is painted over again when dry. 'Joints' can be added to simulate blocks, using 5mm/¼in masking tape to mark out 'mortar lines', painting and peppering over and then removing the masking tape before the last coat. It is best to use a single colour rather than combining this treatment with broken colour effects.

The Influence of Italian Architecture

The builders, craftsmen and decorators who produced houses for the new middle classes of the eighteenth century had a common source of inspiration – the work of Italian Renaissance architects, in particular that of Andrea Palladio (1508–80). The style and appearance of the interiors they created – which were to become the norm for domestic detailing and decoration – were a direct result of their enthusiasm for Palladio's work. The English architect Inigo Jones (1573–1652), who had visited Italy a generation after Palladio's death, was the first to bring this classical language to Britain. But Jones' enthusiasm did not reach its fruition until a century later when Lord Burlington (1695–1753), William Kent (1685–1748) and others resurrected this style with such effect that Palladianism became the basis of much of the architectural and decorative work produced in the British Isles and North America during the next hundred years.

Palladio's buildings are deceptively simple. Based on a strict system of proportions, they make use of plain materials such as stone and plastered

A severely Neoclassical room has white joinery toning with the real white marble of the mantelpiece. The painting of the walls, in a cool, neutral tone, also has an intriguing delicate marble effect. This treatment, combined with the hard surface of the inlaid floor and the huge, light-reflecting looking glass, makes a light and airy room.

Sir John Soane's distinctive use of mouldings is unmistakeable. This architecturally modelled wall, painted a dead white and subject to a strong shaft of light, with a flash of colour from the glass, produces an object lesson in the role of shadow, highlights and perspective, an understanding of which is so important when painting rooms in imitation of stone. Light coming from the top means that all tops and right-hand edges of blocks catch highlights while all left-hand and lower edges cast shadows. The right-hand reveal of the arch, although in shade, has reflected light on it, making it paler than the shaded back wall.

The shade of white paint chosen for the Stony Room is important. A modern, brilliant white does not produce a stony effect.

brick. Most are villas (that is, country houses incorporating farms and living accommodation for owners and servants), rather than grand palaces, and so the ideas they embody translated easily to a smaller scale and to other parts of the world.

Palladianism was ideally expressed in a monochrome tonal palette. Patterns and textures were not, of course, excluded, but this stoniness was, and remains, essential to the style. Stone colours – and they were referred to as such – were the standard treatment for service rooms, hallways, stairs and passages, although they were sometimes extended to other areas. Since these earthy, sandy or grey shades all originate from earth pigments, they were readily available and cheap, factors which encouraged their widespread use. The more expensive, bright colours were reserved for the more important rooms, where their brilliance and value could be displayed to full effect. The neutral quality of the surrounding areas served to emphasize the sumptuousness of the drawing room. Stone itself was a preferred Palladian building material and stone effects, particularly trompe stone blocks, are especially appropriate in the entrance hallways of eighteenth-century houses, where they ease the transition from outside to inside, in a sense referring back to the rustication of the lower storey.

As a natural material, subject to change over time, stone had a particular appeal in the late eighteenth century: it was romantic and symbolized a connection with nature, a connection that the rising industrial age threatened to sever. At the same time, ancient stonework had overtones of history, continuity and stability. A deep reverence for antiquity prevailed in this age which saw the amassing of great private and public collections.

Robert Adam (1728–92) and his friend Giambattista Piranesi (1720–78) were among those who measured, recorded and reconstructed on paper the 'Grandeur that was Rome' and the 'Glory that was Greece'. Piranesi's records of the great Roman ruins are immeasurably enriched by the mass of detail of broken stone, of creepers, bushes, ivy and even of later peasants' huts, squalid in reality but in a visual sense, picturesque. What stone expressed in a wider social context was a way of holding onto the past and allaying a fear of change.

Paradoxically, while the attraction of stone was its simplicity, the use of stone was far from simple. Great effort and elaboration were used to produce an apparently simple decorative language. These 'simple', 'natural' effects are the outcome of great skill and artifice. The same paradox can be seen in the fascination with grottoes – equally artificial features in highly controlled 'natural' landscapes. Very popular in the eighteenth century, these follies required considerable ingenuity and engineering skill to build.

ABOVE *This design of the 1760s by J.L. Clérisseau for a loggia in the convent of S. Trinita dei Monti in Rome exemplifies the romantic attitude to antiquity which was a potent force throughout the second half of the eighteenth century. (The room executed from the design still survives.) The furniture was designed to look like fragments of ancient stonework, with a sarcophagus serving as a 'desk' and a fireplace that could be an ad-hoc arrangement thrown together by squatters.*

RIGHT *The ceiling of the Ruin Room in the Italian watchtower (see page 40) shows a delightful recreation of Clérisseau's design. The skilful handling of light, shade and colour faithfully reproduces the spirit of the watercolour design, without slavishly copying it.*

SIMULATING STONE BLOCKS

One of the simplest ways of simulating stone is to paint lines on the wall to divide it into blocks. The lines should be thought of as mortar joints.

When marking out the blocks it is obviously important to follow the conventional way of building a wall, staggering them in courses. The lining itself can be very simple, using off-white paint and a thin lining brush; or it can be made more elaborate by putting shadows above and highlights below each mortar joint. The next step in building up to full illusion is to begin to suggest the character of the blocks themselves, putting in cracks, adding little dips and hollows or patches of wear, slight colour variations from one block to another and the suggestion of faint veinings. Dummy arches and keystones can be painted over doors and windows to add to the effect. For this type of illusion to be successful, it is important that the cracks and irregularities in the stone account for only a small proportion of the whole area. Restraint and subtlety are far more convincing than over-elaboration. Any very illusionist paintwork also needs to be viewed from a distance to be properly appreciated, so a hallway is often too narrow for this type of treatment, unless it is handled with an extremely light touch.

Rustication and ageing

Simple painted 'stonework' can be worked up in various ways to enliven the surface and lend realism. The upper part of this sample shows fake rustication, and the lower part has been 'aged'.

To achieve these effects, begin in both cases by painting a thin glaze of raw umber and yellow ochre in oil or watercolour over white. Measure out the 'blocks' and pencil them in.

To create the deeply recessed joints of rustication, add shadows in the glaze first used, darkened with a little more raw umber, and paint highlights in white glaze. Signs of ageing are painted freely, using very thin washes of glaze in raw umber and yellow ochre, before the rustication. After the rustication is added, one or two of the shadows or highlights may need strengthening where they cross the 'joints'.

A TROMPE L'OEIL STONE CHEMINÉE WITH MOULDED PANEL

Skilful faking is sometimes admired more than its 'authentic' counterpart, and sleight of hand perhaps enthralls most when the concept as well as the fake finish is so in keeping that it seems almost unimaginable that the room could have been treated in any other way. The unusual and awkward position – across the corner of a room – of this plain and rather ungainly little bedroom fireplace singles it out for special decorative treatment. The whole corner wall has been transformed into a French provincial stone *cheminée*, complete with a moulded panel over the mantelshelf.

In creating a stony finish, layers of translucent colour are built up stage by stage over a white-painted background, and this stony surface is then given 'joints' to make it look like stone blocks. To fake the raised and fielded trompe panel and its mouldings, shadows and highlights are added to a simple outline (see opposite, and page 49). The secret of success lies in restraint rather than elaboration. Here a dense water-based paint was used for the sake of speed, as traditional oil glazes demand long drying times. The work should be allowed to dry thoroughly before each new stage is begun.

A

1 Paint a white background in eggshell. Make a paint glaze using raw umber enlivened with yellow ochre and brush it loosely and evenly over the prepared surface (A).

2 Pencil in lines to suggest stone blocks and outlines of the 'panel' and its 'mouldings' and then strengthen and make these permanent with raw umber, used thinly (B).

B

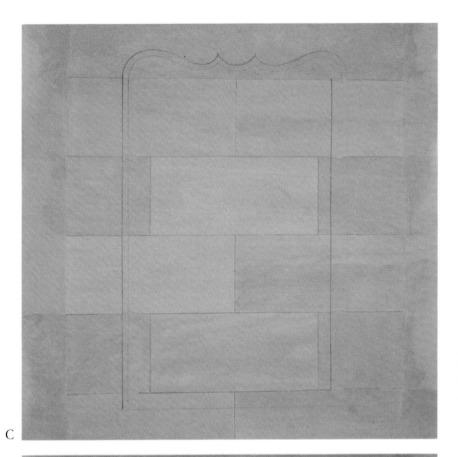

C

3 When this painting is dry give the individual 'blocks' character by adding very light washes of raw umber paint glaze (C) – any streakiness should be kept more or less horizontal.

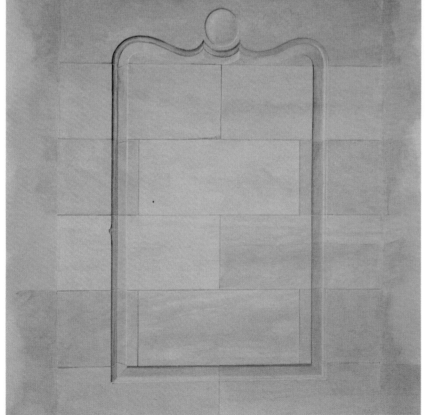

D

4 Add shadows in raw umber and highlights in white (D) to emphasize the 'moulding' round the panel. More work can be done on the 'stone' in raw umber to add extra veining or shadows.

5 Finish off with an almost invisibly white paint glaze to even out and reduce contrasts (RIGHT). When this is dry, varnish with flat varnish. Here the frieze was painted in burnt sienna and stencilled in white to finish off.

RIGHT *Painted lines are the simplest way of making a stone wall and can easily be reproduced in printed wallpaper. No pretence of stoniness has been made in this wallpaper, other than the rigorous and convincing pattern of course upon course of blocks.*

LEFT *'Stony' techniques work well in hallways, marking the transition from outside to inside. Here the upper part of the wall is marbled in raw sienna (as was the tradition in row houses) and burnt sienna has been introduced as a decorative feature on the dado and door.*

RIGHT *An ambitious stone finish was sought for this room. The old plaster had already been incised with lines but more contrast was wanted, so shadows and highlights were painted on each block to make the walls look like rusticated stonework (as shown on page 52). The colours of the trompe panels below the windows and the huge fanciful shell overdoors were kept within the general colour and tonal range of the walls, while the cornice and baseboard were deliberately painted to be richer and shiny.*

This lime-ash floor, dating from the sixteenth century, has, like the eighteenth-century dado and baseboard, been marbled in a limited palette. I varnished the unpainted centre of the floor and gave a surround of white paint with veins. The baseboard fascia is of pale grey with darker veins, and the dado is white with darker veins. All the veining is done into wet paint except for some of the fine detail on the dado.

MARBLE, GRANITE AND SLATE

Marble is incredibly varied in colour, structure and texture. Many of the highly coloured kinds feature in complex inlaid and patterned schemes and have little in common with the qualities of the Stony Room as it appears in this chapter. However, those qualities of cool dryness with echoes of Italy that characterize the Stony Room are well expressed in some of the simpler kinds of marble. In this case the patterning of the marble will be less important than its cool translucency – and the process of simulating it in paint is not intended to reproduce the material realistically, but to give a suggestion of these qualities – a much more painterly interpretation.

In faking a marble finish on the walls of a stony room, it is important to study the real material, rather than a marbled finish, and to use this for reference. If it is possible to generalize, it could be said that the

Marbling for the Stony Room

This type of marbling mimics the stone in a general and rather free manner.

In the first sample (RIGHT, ABOVE), the effects of steps 1–4 are shown building up from left to right, illustrating how subtly the work is changed. The colours used for the glaze are raw umber and yellow ochre mixed with white. Each stage is added when the previous one is dry.

1 Using a soft watercolour brush, paint bands of thin glaze onto a white background. Soften and blend them to give a massing of dark and light.

2 Paint in veins which intersect and flow apart again, getting thicker and thinner by turns. The veins should follow the direction of the bands, breaking off to cross them at shallow angles from time to time.

3 Apply a second coat of veining to strengthen the effect.

4 Add a little more raw umber to the glaze to darken it and paint in more and finer veining.

In the second sample (RIGHT, BELOW) a stronger pattern and colour are given to this work, using the same glaze, to which a little burnt umber has been added.

1 Brush over a thin oil glaze following the existing rhythms. Soften with a badger blender (left-hand side of sample).

2 While the glaze is wet, spatter and draw in a few veins with turpentine or white spirit. Pass the softener gently over these areas to reveal the underpainting (right-hand side of sample). Work in one direction so that the glaze will heap up on one edge to give the impression of shadow.

distinguishing characteristic of marble is the arrangement of veins that cross and re-cross the surface, sometimes widening into fissures, unlike the veins of other types of stone, which run parallel to each other. It is crucial to understand the original material as this makes it possible to give a deft, accurate suggestion of the pattern which makes all the difference to the final result.

Once the real marble surface has been studied it would be best put away and its essentials concentrated on. Both tools and palette should be kept simple, avoiding fussy effects with pheasant feathers or sponges and concentrating instead on translucency and depth through a series of glazes and overlays, all based on tones of stony colour.

Slate – most appropriate for baseboards, though usable almost anywhere – is a way of introducing a near black into stony rooms, to sharpen up the scheme. Granite effects are examples of the richest patterning applicable to this kind of room where relaxed rhythms, subtle colours and smooth textures are the norm. However, the use of granite in subdued colours and lightly spattered – as opposed to sponged – is a good example of the use of stronger rhythms in stony rooms.

ABOVE *This nineteenth-century panelled pilaster is spattered in paler greys over a darker background and the picture clearly shows the impossibility of getting the spatters to go into the hollow portions of the moulding. The central panel has been marbled in a sienna colour. The final glaze was lifted off with solvent in places to create veins (as shown on page 59), while the darker, greyish, veins were worked into the earlier coat.*

RIGHT *The affinity of water and stone makes stony and marbled paint effects favourite choices for bathrooms. This neat little room, intensely detailed and highly finished in granite-like speckled stone and veined marble has been varnished, both for practical reasons and to produce a precise finish. It is at once simple and complex and its richness is not compromised by over-elaboration.*

Simulating slate

The range of contrast in slate (BELOW) is very limited, so subtlety is needed. The work is done in the following stages.

1 The background is painted in an appropriate slate colour first. Here a flat black was used and allowed to dry.

2 White glaze is brushed on very thinly in soft bands and a few spatters are also added. A paler version of the background colour can be used instead of white for this stage.

3 Using a badger blender, these marks are softened – in one direction only – so that they look like the cloudy bands present in the natural material.

4 A few tiny, very pale veins can be introduced. This can be done when the work is still wet or after it is dry. At each stage all the work should flow in one direction.

ABOVE *Everything in this neatly detailed little room has been given a spattered granite finish. At this date (c. 1800) spattering (see page 39) was used both for porphyry (on a dark purply-blue background) and for granite (here on a pink ground). Later in the nineteenth century, sponging was more often used for granite. Here, the spattering is done in off-white and black and the walls are lined out to resemble blocks. Strangely, the cornice has been whitewashed with the ceiling – though this may well be a later repaint. The joinery in this room is grained to simulate oak.*

MOULDINGS

From Palladio and his followers comes a distinctive use of mouldings, whether in stone, plaster or wood – a language that seems best expressed in terms of stoniness. The mouldings relate to classical precedent and to their use in Roman architecture. The wall is divided into horizontal bands. From the top down, the cornice, frieze and architrave together form the entablature. The wall surface stands for the columns and their capitals, the chair rail (or dado rail), dado and baseboard correspond to the plinth. In the eighteenth century these divisions and their relative proportions were taken for granted and even today they are implicit if not explicit in most domestic interiors.

The forms of cornices in the eighteenth century were remarkably standardized. Their simple profiles would almost invariably be drawn directly, via the many copybooks and engravings, from classical sources. In the nineteenth century the emphasis of the cornice was spread onto the ceiling and the cast ornament was often naturalistic.

The picture rail, a nineteenth-century invention, was the result of a fusing of the tubular brass rail used for hanging pictures and the architrave that was the lowest member of the entablature. As the century progressed it crept down the wall and, as often as not, the ceiling colour was carried over cornice and frieze in an unclassical way. Classical logic would demand that the cornice be part of the wall, not of the ceiling.

Baseboards in Palladian interiors, bold and simple, were often up to 5cm/2in thick, even in comparatively small rooms, clearly revealing their stone ancestry. Later, in the nineteenth century, they were to become slighter (though often taller) and reveal more of the joiner's hand. Indeed, the Palladian convention was to paint the flat part of the baseboard in a dark slate colour, as against the late eighteenth- and early nineteenth-century fashion for white joinery.

Whether you propose to paint real mouldings as if they were stone or whether you want to paint illusionist mouldings that look like stone, it is important to consider what could have been made in stone and what could not. Bigger, bolder details would be much easier to achieve in stone and are, anyway, more in keeping with the sense of strength and stability implicit in the Stony Room.

RIGHT *This segment of trompe l'oeil entablature demonstrates the way in which real and trompe stone can be ornamented or left virtually plain. The left-hand part of this example is painted to represent plain mouldings (with the cross-section indicated as a line drawing), while the right-hand section shows how extra work can be done to enrich some of the mouldings with decorative details.*

I glazed the background in yellow ochre and raw umber and worked the mouldings in raw umber, with white added in places. Using a broad lining brush and a straight edge, the mouldings were built up in washes of colour, starting with a dark tone. Once all the middle to dark tones were done and blended the darkest and lightest lines were added. To prevent the contrast being too strong on any part of the mouldings a darker or lighter wash can be used along the whole length. It is better to aim for lighter rather than darker effects.

BELOW *A piece of architrave is painted dark grey and glazed with white. The white glaze hangs in the hollows and is dragged off the top of the mouldings. The effect is of old stone dust settled into cracks.*

THE PATTERNED ROOM

If we think of decoration first in terms of colour, our second consideration is usually pattern. Pattern is a way of enriching surfaces by an arrangement of elements of colour, motif or texture. Although the details themselves may not be repeated, there will always be a rhythm to the arrangement. The history of pattern in fabric, paper and paint provides a fertile source of ideas for decorators today, and the revival and adaptation of patterns is at the heart of this history.

PATTERNS IN TEXTILES, PAINT AND PAPER

Patterned fabric and painted designs were used on walls in medieval times, and patterned papers have existed since the fifteenth century. The decorative tapestries of the noble medieval courts were richly patterned with figurative designs. They, in turn, were imitated in paint on walls and on heavy woollen cloth. Tapestries could be hung quite simply from loops or on rods as 'hangings' (and so could be easily moved), or were stretched over battens. This technique, with its implications of permanency, has been used ever since, not only for tapestry and other woven finishes but also for wallpaper.

The earliest wallpapers were stencilled or handprinted with bold, often heraldic motifs or stylized floral patterns reflecting the designs of woven cloth. In the seventeenth century this imitation of cloth became even more realistic with the introduction of flock papers designed to look like damask weaves and made by shaking wool or silk trimmings onto a pattern which was block-printed in paste over a coloured background. The underside of the paper was then beaten to make the 'pile' stand up. At this time wallpaper was produced in fairly small pieces and was used in much the same way as textiles, often mounted on scrim (a kind of canvas) stretched over wooden battens pinned to the walls.

Papers imported from China from the late seventeenth century onward depicting landscapes of trees, birds and flowering shrubs or scenes of oriental life, although they have no repeating elements, have a rhythm of scale and spacing that makes a pattern. Papers in imitation of cloth, whether in tones of the same colour or in contrasting colour schemes, and Chinese papers, whether real imports or local copies, were to remain important in decorating throughout the eighteenth century.

Pattern at its simplest is introduced in this interior with the nearly regular arrangement of big, freehand dots of black paint. This is a repainting of the original eighteenth-century decoration and shows the most direct way of breaking up a plain wall with materials that can readily be found (the black paint used originally was probably soot). The plain beams, deep baseboards and simple shapes are well served by the boldness of the decoration.

The early nineteenth century added its own panoramic landscapes –
nearer to tapestry in the rhythm of the arrangement of their elements
than to naturalistic representation. These were particularly popular in
France and North America, and the characteristic motifs of each new
revival or enthusiasm of the period would in turn become the focus of
new designs.

Throughout this period, walls without paper or cloth hangings,
sometimes even if panelled, were colourwashed and stencilled with
repeating patterns or occasionally painted with narrative scenes. From
the late eighteenth century, stencilling was popular in areas where
fashionable papers, while not unknown, were prohibitively expensive.
It had a particular appeal in America and it is to American stencil designs
that most successful modern work refers. But handpainted or block-
printed designs with repeated motifs all have a stylized appearance and
provide inspiration for modern stencilling.

ABOVE *The distinctive, colourful
patterns of flame stitch on the
upholstery and wallhanging of this
seventeenth-century room are in scale
with the small size of the panels. The
embroidered fabric hangs in folds in
medieval style.*

RIGHT *The rich Baroque patterns of
stamped, gilded and painted leather
provided visual interest in the candle-
and firelit rooms of the seventeenth and
eighteenth century, as did the bold
mouldings of the joinery with their
deep shadows.*

LEFT The typical French toile de Jouy is essentially an all-over pattern. Rather than dominating, its motifs give an even coverage and density. Yet these can easily be isolated, to be used by the upholsterer for chair seats and backs, where the drawing of the details is elegant and admirable for itself.

BELOW This early nineteenth-century wallpaper imitates oriental fabrics which had a diaper pattern woven into the cloth, and were overpainted with trailing, flowering branches. The idea of fabric is emphasized by the border, which is used as if to hide the fabric edges at the joins.

As the eighteenth century progressed, damasks and brocades were to be supplanted by lighter patterns and fabrics as printed cottons and linens, in sprigged and flowered designs, became available. Chintz patterns represent a curious and particular hybrid between the naturalistic strand of Chinese figurative designs and typical repeating patterns. The term, derived from the Sanskrit for 'gaily coloured', was applied to textiles printed or painted in India and imported to the West, and since the days of its early popularity chintz has remained an indispensable part of the decorating vocabulary. The patterns are arranged for production purposes in a regular way, but with the pattern repeat disguised so that the flowers and plants seem to cover the entire surface in an organic way.

While fabrics were still used on walls, printed wallpapers, in a variety of repeated motifs in designs reflecting those of the fabrics, became increasingly popular. Fine, expensive or handpainted papers were sometimes set out in panels and trimmed with a border or braid as if they were fabric.

In the 1830s the wallpaper industry experienced a boom as technology and the market kept pace with each other. This neat, regular but quite assertive pattern in arsenic green and off-white is typical of the European Biedermeier style of this time. The elaborate trompe l'oeil frieze of softly pleated 'cloth' – one of hundreds of versions from this period – is a reminder of the fabric origins of wallpapers.

The mid-nineteenth century, with its bright, chemical colours from coal-tar dyes, saw the introduction of machine-produced paper and the use of wallpaper proliferated. Continuous rolls of paper were first manufactured in the 1830s. Previously, wallpaper lengths had been made up of sheets pasted together before printing. The introduction of both continuous paper and continuous printing meant that the new mass market, eager for new patterns and designs, could be satisfied.

If a dado existed, the main paper was hung only on the upper part of the wall, but the dado itself might also be papered, in a plainer design. The last quarter of the century saw the introduction of heavily textured and embossed papers, which became popular for decorating below the chair rail, especially in areas like hallways and stairs where smooth plaster would show up any damage to the surface.

This was a time of eclecticism, and many interiors, burdened by layers of rich patterning in papers, curtains, carpets and ornaments, would have exhibited an ill-digested assemblage of styles and influences. But from the 1860s onwards, William Morris and similarly minded artist-craftsmen began to reintroduce traditionally block-printed papers, cottons and linens, and woven woollen fabrics in deliberately two-dimensional designs and fresh colours. Inspired by medieval designs, or by the natural world, some of these Arts and Crafts designs capture the feel of flat stencilled work, some of Eastern-inspired chintzes, and often their patterns have a fresh, flowing character which was revolutionary for the time.

Pattern makers in the William Morris tradition continued to produce new designs into the twentieth century. Many of these, or designs derived from them, as well as Morris's own designs, are still in production in their original colours as well as in new 'fashionable' colours, giving a wide choice of fabrics and papers.

Old tapestry (used on the sofa) and oriental rugs share many of the qualities admired by William Morris and constantly referred to in his designs. The curtains are in a Morris fabric. The stripped pine panelling is harmonious in colour and tone, but is in modern taste and would have been as unknown to William Morris as it was in the eighteenth century.

Types of Pattern

Most patterns repeat regularly over the surface, with some taking care not to show the repeat to give an overall effect. Many regularly repeating patterns, such as stripes and checks, gingham and plaid, derive from weaving. The often self-coloured pattern copied directly from Baroque silk or woollen damasks, very different in character, also has its origin in textiles. These designs have a rich effect quite unlike the rather homespun simplicity of stripes and checks. Moiré or animal skin patterns, like the marks that result from colourwashing, ragging or marbling, have a rhythmic and random pattern of their own. Figurative patterns may or may not repeat and, as in the design of Chinese wallpaper, they may repeat over such a large area that the repeat is often lost. In other designs, the repetition of the pattern, however small the scale, is disguised, so that, as in chintz, the overall effect is of flowers and plants interwoven without repeating.

Some patterns are insistent and demanding of attention; others are subtle and retiring. This is partly a question of scale, and partly one of colour – a Chinese pictorial paper is attention demanding, even in subtle colours, because of its scale and content, while the boldest stripes in subtle colours can make a subtle statement.

PATTERN BLENDING

Bold, insistent patterns generally need to be complemented by muted surfaces. In Adam rooms, an intricately patterned carpet or inlaid floor was often echoed by an ornately decorated ceiling, but the walls were kept comparatively plain. When pattern is used on several of the room's surfaces it needs to be carefully handled – as it was in the eighteenth-century application of damask, with its rich, strong patterns; the same fabric might be used for curtains, walls and upholstered furniture so that there were no competing areas of attention. Quiet, small-scale patterns, however, usually mix more readily. Many of them may have such a subtle pattern that it verges on texture, the merest modulation of the surface. Most checks and stripes are the pattern equivalent of neutral shades and combine well, both with each other and with other patterns.

To mix other patterns it is often a good idea to look for a common denominator in terms of colour, theme or scale. Kelims, for example, with their rich vegetable colours and folk designs, present a family of patterns that blend well. Because of the technology employed in producing them, the patterning tends to be on a similar scale, which again contributes to their successful blending. By looking for such similarities of colour and scale, it is usually possible to find groups of prints that mix well in the same way.

A library is always richly patterned by the horizontals and verticals of the shelving and the books. To use any obviously striped pattern would therefore be unwise. Here, the striped design of the cotton curtains is disguised partly by the nature of the stripes and partly by the broken folds. The wall has a very different pattern, one of a Baroque damask character that is stencilled in close tones but in a strong colour.

Choosing Patterns

Trellis patterns have to be used with care. It can be difficult to make them work where there are angles to compete with those of the design, but in this room the diagonals of the window wall exactly match those in the intricate French trellis-patterned wallpaper and are echoed in the glazing of the upper sash. The verticals of the matchboarded dado, the striped upholstery, and even the view through the window, allow the sinuous cane furniture to make its own statement.

Geometric patterns, such as stripes or checks, usually work best in regularly shaped rooms where their crisp linearity gives a sense of graphic definition and can help to emphasize the room's edges. A room with many different angles and projections, or uneven plaster, benefits from the use of a less formal, more open pattern that can dissolve the boundaries and draw attention from the room's irregularity. Patterns of a diaper type are best avoided on stairs, where the string of the stairs will almost always be at a different angle from that in the paper. These geometric patterns which derive, as often as not, from the technology of weaving, are similar to the kinds of patterns used for floors in stone, bricks, tiles or lumber. The units of the pattern are inflexible (a grid arrangement is implicit) and yet the designs that can be carried out in rectangular bricks alone seem limitless. Add a second colour, add again a square tile and the possibilities multiply enormously. A diagonal arrangement for a floor pattern will generally add an expanding movement to a room, whereas a straight, rectangular arrangement

implies a more rigid geometry. A contrasting border will demand a clear floor plan, while an 'invisible' border, with perhaps a central emphasis to the floor, will suit an irregular room.

It is generally accepted that small patterns should be used in small rooms and that large patterns belong to large rooms, but the scale of the pattern and the scale of the room can often be contrasted to pleasing effect. William Morris advocated that small rooms could benefit from large patterns, where the pattern may even cease to read as a pattern and may be interpreted as a motif. In the same way, although small patterns are usually avoided in large rooms on the grounds that the eye reads over the pattern on a large area and cannot distinguish its elements, this effect can be very welcome, with the pattern virtually disappearing and the overall impression being almost that of a texture.

A simple room has been simply distempered and enlivened with a neat little stencil which produces the effect of tiling. In its regularity and formality, the design is in happy contrast with the relaxed effect of stencilling on rough plaster.

To enable the pattern to go right into the corner, the stencil is cut or folded and the adjacent wall masked while working. These finishing touches are done after the main work is completed.

A traditional floor pattern that is still much produced is one of the simplest geometric patterns, the typically Dutch black and white chequerboard. On the early American floorcloth (BELOW) the design is painted on canvas and then covered with many coats of varnish. Floorcloths like this are the precursors of linoleum.

RIGHT The three-dimensional effect of 'tumbling blocks' is created in Italian ceramic floor tiles in three different tones. The tiles are all of the same shape and size. This illusionist trick is based on a long tradition dating back at least to Roman mosaic pavements. The same pattern is often found in marble tiles and in inlaid wood and patchwork.

ABOVE This wooden floor is painted to imitate an eighteenth-century dot pattern floor in Portland stone and slate. I painted shadows and highlights to throw the diagonal slates into convincing relief, since, being of a more durable nature, they show less wear than the white slabs. This type of floor pattern is still popular, and can be found in linoleum and vinyl floor tiles.

USING FABRIC

Fabrics can rival even the best wallpapers and since simple fabrics are also often cheaper than good papers there is every reason to use them as a wall covering. Fabric makes a rich surface. When applied over a layer of interlining (which provides an even surface on which to mount the fabric) it is warm to the touch and can also help to deaden sound and to insulate a room, which is why it was first used as a wall covering. These qualities make it particularly good for use in bedrooms, or wherever a sense of enclosure is wanted. Because of the obvious cleaning problems, fabric is not suitable for rooms where it is likely to be splashed with water or grease, or exposed to smoke.

Although fabric can be used with extravagance and complexity, pleated or ruched (which, with the rhythmic folds that result, gives even plain fabric a pattern), or caught up with decorative bosses and hooks in Empire style for a lighter, less permanent effect, the more usual way is stretched flat on the wall so that the pattern, weave or texture is displayed. It is perhaps best set off against a dado and defined by braiding (which also covers raw edges), in the eighteenth-century manner. Silk damasks have an incomparably rich look but printed or woven patterns in cotton or other cheaper fabrics can also produce good walling. Fabric can be pasted direct to the wall, as it is or paper-backed, but the traditional method of stretching it over battens and interlining produces the best results.

In this small, densely-packed bedroom I wanted to use fabric to create a patterned room that nevertheless gave due prominence to the patterns of the Moroccan black and gold mirror and the Indian printed cotton hanging. So, for the walls, curtains and bedhangings, I used several different patterns, all of a similar scale, none of which is to be thought of as much more than a texture.

The cloth used for the walling is a red and black cotton chintz. The black all-over pattern gently enriches the surface and the interlined cloth insulates the room. The curtains, fringed to match the wall braid, carry a second all-over pattern, but in this case one that is geometric. The tester and bed curtains – all lined in plain cotton – have a different geometric pattern. The use of geometric patterns for folded surfaces helps to balance them with the comparatively irregular pattern on the walls.

MOUNTING FABRIC ON A WALL

In the eighteenth century fabric walling was so much the norm that battens on which to mount it were often let in flush with the surface of the wall. Today they are simply screwed or tacked to the wall around the perimeter, with extra battens fixed vertically or horizontally where pictures are to be hung. An interlining is stapled or tacked to the battens and trimmed to fit, and the fabric is then stapled or tacked on top. Finally the fabric edges are trimmed and the staples or tacks are hidden by braid, ribbon or gimp, or by a carved and gilded or painted wooden fillet. If the corners are to be braid- or fillet-free, the fabric may be fixed with back-tacking strip (as shown in the illustrations here) – a stiff card that is also used in upholstering furniture. When several widths of fabric are needed to cover the wall, the fabric is cut generously to length and the widths joined, right sides together, using a flat seam and with the pattern carefully matched across the seams. Fabric (and lining) should be stretched smooth but not overstretched. Any painting is done before the fabric is applied.

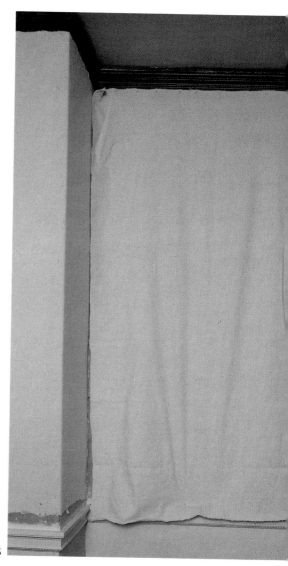

A

B

1 Make a framework for the fabric using plywood strips 6mm/¼in thick and 5cm/2in wide. (Measure each length separately, as the distance from dado to ceiling and the width from wall to wall may vary slightly across the room.) Fix the strips all round the perimeter of each wall surface, using screws and wall plugs or tacks and adhesive (A). The battens must be fixed securely as the cloth stretched across them imposes considerable strain. Fix additional strips if necessary for hanging pictures. Use a spirit level to make sure that these strips are straight.

2 Cut lining to size, allowing 2.5–5cm/1–2in extra all round. Seam widths as necessary to make the pieces large enough. Attach the lining to the wall battens, starting at the middle of the top edge. Use tacks or staples to fix the lining loosely, as you smooth it out towards the edges without stretching it. Smooth the lining down towards the bottom and fix it to match the top (B). Smooth and loosely fix the sides, and finally the corners, as shown on the finished section of wall to the left.

3 Fix the lining firmly in place all round. Trim the edges neatly (C).

4 Cut and seam together vertically sufficient widths of the top fabric to cover each wall, allowing an additional 5–10cm/2–4in top and bottom for trimming. Match the pattern carefully.

5 Cut a length of back-tacking strip for each inner corner.

6 Start in a corner of the room for each stretch of wall. Place one vertical edge of fabric right side down, sandwiched against the wall under the back-tacking strip (D). Secure to the batten by stapling through all layers (E).

C

D

E

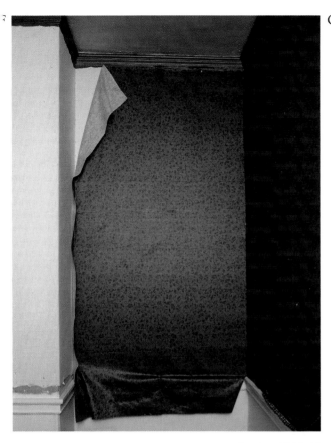

7 Strain the bulk of the fabric sideways over the back-tacking strip and across the wall. Hold it in place along the top and bottom with temporary staples.

8 When the fabric is smooth and taut, staple it in place, beginning in the middle and working alternately up and down (F). Leave a few centimetres of fabric free all round.

9 Remove the temporary staples. Finish off the corners (G). Begin the next area as in step 6.

10 Finally, trim all raw edges and cover them with braid, securing it with wallpaper adhesive, which is quick-drying, non-staining and easy to apply from a tube. Apply the adhesive to the braid and hold it temporarily in place with a few staples until the adhesive dries (H).

Most modern wallpapers, even when they are otherwise faithful reproductions of old papers, lack an essential quality found in the original: in the eighteenth century, the pattern was handprinted using distemper paints and wooden printing blocks. Not only did the paint have discernible thickness – giving the paper a tactile quality which is entirely lost in modern papers printed in inks which have little or no thickness – but also the way the colour left the block was clearly visible, producing tiny sub-patterns on the areas of colour. Flock papers are perhaps less disappointing substitutes. Although flocked papers could be in strong colour contrasts, especially in the later eighteenth century, when flocking might be in blue on cream, russet on green or crimson on yellow, flocking is particularly effective in one colour, or shades of one colour, making it look like damask or cut velvet.

To recapture the tactile quality that is sadly missing from most modern papers, it is worth experimenting with other types of paper and paper patterning – with stencilling and paint techniques and print rooms (see the Collector's Room, pages 176–9). Almost any kind of paper can be stuck to the wall. One original example was a room entirely papered in front pages of *The Times*, in the days when the front page was devoted to columns of classified advertisements. Each page, trimmed of its margins, was carefully stuck to the wall so that the columns gave the effect of a striped paper. Other papers with surface qualities that would give interest and delight include brown wrapping paper and almost any handmade paper, such as Japanese grass or mulberry papers. Specialist paper shops have a wide range of papers in many different sizes and finishes. The final effect results from the surface grain and texture of the

The reproduction of historic papers is seldom so successful or authentic in both methods and materials as in these two examples. In the first (LEFT) an eighteenth-century baroque damask pattern is block-printed in distemper colours on a handbrushed ground. The texture and nature of the paint are most evident in the white printing, which provides a tiny minor pattern, an enrichment within the bold formality of the main design. The second (RIGHT) is a geometric design – also based on weaving – of interlaced circles. Reproducing a design which dates from the second half of the eighteenth century, it is printed in flock on a handbrushed ground.

Both patterns were based on woven fabrics and would typically have been used with a border or fillet as though they were indeed fabric.

paper used, as well as from the size of the individual sheets and how they are laid – perhaps in grid fashion or in staggered courses. Although some of the textural effects may be lost if the surface is sealed, varnish can be used to seal the paper, either to give a shiny finish with added richness and reflections, or to waterproof it if, for example, it is used in a bathroom. A difficulty with varnishing paper is that oil in the varnish has an immediate yellowing effect on the paper which may be unwanted. The answer is to seal the paper with size or a water-based varnish first, applying the protective oil-based varnish when this is completely dry. Varnish exaggerates surface imperfections and is therefore not suitable for use on any paper which has been applied specifically to cover such irregularities.

A set of nineteenth-century prints has been stuck in regular rows, edge to edge, so that the prints entirely cover the walls above the dark panelled dado of this bedroom. Despite the fact that the prints are very different from one another, the size and shape of each image and the widths of the borders provide a rhythm.

USING PAINT

Many of the patterns one can create in paint fall into the category of small-scale designs, which verge on the textural and are similar in effect to fabrics woven with tiny decorative motifs, or to fabrics with obvious open weaves such as canvas or burlap, perhaps belonging more to the Coloured than to the Patterned Room. Some paint techniques, however, produce much more obvious non-repeating patterns. Spattering, in which flecks of paint are knocked off the end of a brush onto a surface to give a fine, regular, speckled pattern, is one of these (see the Coloured Room, page 39).

There is also a type of marbling that falls into the category of rich, painted patterns. Unlike the marbling described in the Stony Room (pages 58–60) and the Panelled Room (page 109), this kind of marbling is detailed, intensely coloured, and often set out in geometric or figurative arrangements which simulate opulent inlaid surfaces. Colours can be quite bright – rich greens and reds, rather than pale greys and off-whites. As in other forms of marbling, it is important to study a real example before attempting any form of imitation. The patterning here is more detailed and insistent, but the result should not be crude or brash. While the aim will be to imitate contrasting colours and types of marble, the palette within each colour should be restricted to a natural and limited range of tones.

This marbling technique is similar to those already described, but a

RIGHT The tiny abstract pattern of spattering is linked here to the regular rhythm of vertical boarding. Although the wall finish imitates porphyry there is really no intention of concealing the inherent woodiness of this typical nineteenth-century Swedish house. The use of a small, irregular pattern in confined areas, which are vulnerable to wear, has many practical benefits.

LEFT The rich and varied abstract patterns of Baroque marbling are full of rhythms – some intricate, as on the panels of this door, some bold and measured, as in the dado and door surround. Here, complex rhythms of pattern, surface and colour are set off, but not swamped, by plain painted crimson walls.

broader range of tools and methods is needed to stress its particular decorative patterning. Here, the background can be ragged or sponged to give a mottled, clouded look, and veins and fissures can either be drawn on with a fine brush or feather or taken out with a solvent and a softener. To give the pattern a textured look, and create a lively surface rather than a flat impression, the work can be spattered with pigment, or, conversely, 'cissed' with solvent.

Patterns in paint can of course be created by freehand work but for many, stencilling is one of the most satisfactory ways of using paint to create a Patterned Room. Stencilling reappeared in the mainstream of decoration relatively recently, as part of the revival of interest in traditional country life and handicrafts. Part of its appeal is that the effect of wallpaper or fabric can be imitated using colours and patterns that may not be readily available. And, with stencilling, the pattern can be adapted to fit the space, suiting the scale of the pattern to the scale of the room and accommodating irregularities by adjusting the spacing.

One feature of modern stencilling, not found in original examples, is the use of shading within each individual part of the stencil, often achieved by spray-painting rather than brushwork. Unfortunately, the results are not always successful and freshness and vitality, the great virtues of the traditional method, are lost. To achieve the strong graphic appeal of the real thing it is best to go back to tradition and concentrate on achieving solid blocks of colour.

Stencilling is especially associated with the early North American settlers such as the Pennsylvania Dutch, who evolved their own characteristic motifs of hearts, tulips, leaves and geometric shapes although such patterns and techniques were not exclusive to North America and examples are found throughout Europe.

These folk patterns were largely executed in a limited range of colours on white or pale-coloured distempered backgrounds. Distemper, being a very absorbent surface, took up the paint quickly. The stencils themselves, stylized in a fashion that made them easy to cut, were made from stiff materials such as leather, thin metal or varnished paper and scaled to the size of the hand. The effect of the finished work was typically flat and graphic, with blocks of colour and no tonal gradations, but nevertheless with the almost imperceptible irregularity that comes from working by hand using natural materials. Not only walls, but also floors and furniture were stencilled. A different source of ideas for stencillers comes from the Gothic Revival stencilling that was used in Victorian church decoration. Here patterns are in a revived medieval style, with heraldic imagery and strong colours.

Another type of stencilling which is also part of a long tradition, although it creates a much more sophisticated effect, seeks to duplicate the density of a patterned fabric such as damask. Many of these motifs are symmetrical, and can be made with one stencil used twice, flipped over for the second printing. Before cutting, plan the pattern so that the stencil will be the right size to fit a given number of repeats from top to bottom of the wall. When the background and stencilling are close in colour the result is a textured look, while quite different effects can be achieved using contrasting colours.

RIGHT *The characteristics, colours and finishes of early nineteenth-century Swedish decoration are unmistakeable. The picture shows a stencilled pattern related to contemporary wallpaper and fabrics in the form of densely packed and richly ornamented stripes.*

BELOW *Cork tiles are a quick, cheap and easily applied covering for bathroom floors, but can appear bland. For this floor, I cut two stencils, which are regularly arranged but irregularly turned one way and another. Casein paint takes easily on unfinished cork. The floor is then varnished with a proprietary cork floor varnish.*

HOW TO STENCIL

There are many pre-cut stencils on the market, but it is often more satisfying to cut original stencils, using stencil card or Mylar (a plastic film). Modern stencil card is a heavy, oiled paper which can be drawn on and cut with a sharp knife. Mylar has the advantage of being transparent for easy registration of the print but is difficult to draw on and not so easy to cut. To apply the paint you will need a stencilling brush or any round, dense brush cut square – a shaving brush is ideal. A sponge can be used to achieve a faded, broken look.

The method, once the design has been planned, is to hold the stencil against the wall and either brush on the paint or 'pounce' it on with a quick, dabbing motion. The consistency of the paint is vital: if too thin it will run under the stencil, if too thick it will clog it. Try out different consistencies on a prepared surface and practise the techniques before working on the wall.

1 Before beginning to stencil, plan the layout of the pattern on the walls and make registration marks in pencil. This demands a degree of skill, especially if opaque card is being used. The stencils need to be marked with dots or nicks to make sure that the successive prints will line up. You also need to plan the pattern so that it fits coherently into the wall space.

2 Mix paint to the right consistency. Using one colour and one stencil at a time, apply the paint through the stencils working from top to bottom.

ABOVE *The pattern for the stencilling demonstrated here and used to decorate a modern bedroom (see page 91) was inspired by a nineteenth-century American stencilled pattern. A stencil design in the classic American style usually consists of alternating vertical bands – a minor band which is stylized and geometrical, framing a band of more colourful and often larger motifs.*

LEFT *The inspiration for these stencilled patterns (in an early nineteenth-century Swedish house) comes from a variety of sources, their common scale and materials providing visual unity. In the hall the pattern is clearly based on painted tiles and the room seen through the door has a pattern of widely spaced daisy shapes again related to contemporary wallpapers and woven silks, while in the room to the left an Indian printed cotton was probably the model.*

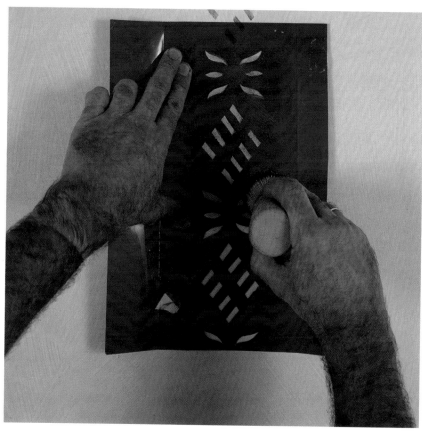

Latex paint or distemper may be used as a background for stencilling. The pattern can be painted in the same type of paint as the background. However, in both these examples I used artists' gouache paints. These come in a good range of colours and can be mixed if the right colour cannot be found. They are thinned with water and they dry quickly. For an authentic look, restrict colours to those that were used originally – yellows, reds, dull greens, or perhaps Prussian blue.

The paint can be pounced or brushed. Pouncing suits distempered walls, the paint sinks rapidly into the absorbent surface to leave a soft, almost mottled print as shown RIGHT, while brushing leaves attractive marks on less absorbent latex surfaces, as shown BELOW, creating a lively effect in which the paint covers the latex unevenly to produce areas of different densities, and therefore intensities, of colour. The result is similar in appearance to some eighteenth-century wallpapers which were block-printed onto a distempered ground and then had colours added by brush through stencils.

RIGHT *The finished room stencilled in this design shows the importance of the structure underlying the openness of the pattern. Without this structure the effect would be chaotic. The minor banding regulates the freer major band, while the wide spacing gives an airy look in contrast to the tighter, more intense design of the American original (page 89). The pattern has been carefully spaced to suit the room, with the minor banding being carried round the arched entrance to the room. Stencilled patterns based on American designs often refer back to fabric and as here, are finished off with a 'trimming' border top and bottom.*

THE PANELLED ROOM

Panelling, as a way of covering bare stone or brick walls, predates the use of plaster as a standard finish in domestic interiors. Fitting an inner skin of wood meant that the room was protected from the elements and provided insulation against damp and cold. Panelling made habitable rooms that might otherwise have been bleak, bare, draughty and unfurnished. The other great advantage of panelling, less tangible, but today perhaps more important than its practical qualities, is its ability to envelop and create a sense of enclosure in a room. At least part of this quality is due to the way panelling softens and absorbs sound, in contrast to the harder, echoing resonance of a plastered room. It is also an effective means of breaking up large surfaces into comfortable, familiar proportions.

Panelling evolved at a time when wood and labour were plentiful and cheap. Today, whatever the wood used, it is no longer an inexpensive choice and its use tends to suggest a certain luxury. The alternative is to simulate the real thing and, indeed, from an early point in decorative history, panelling has been suggested and simulated in a variety of ways. Although faked panelling obviously does not insulate in any way, it does articulate a plain room to pleasing effect.

Traditional Panelling

The many different decorative styles that are handed down to us from the past all have their specific historical associations – their 'period feel'. Panelling reflects, in its diversity of styles, the changing and evolving forms of the different periods from which it comes. Apart from a few surviving medieval planked walls, the earliest examples of panelling in domestic interiors date from the sixteenth century. At this time, panels were quite small (each about 45 × 60cm/18in × 2ft, slightly taller than wide), their size being dictated largely by the available technology: as time went by, individual panels were to become larger. Elaborate examples of early panelling might reflect an Italian influence in their shape; linenfold carving was another form of embellishment. The panels themselves were relatively thin, held in place by vertical stiles and horizontal rails that were morticed and tenoned together to form a

Panelling can take many forms, depending on the age and grandeur or simplicity of the house. In all cases it can emphasize the proportions of the room and make the walls seem 'furnished'. The style of a room's panelling echoes that of its woodwork, but a Panelled Room need not be lined with wood. Instead, trompe l'oeil panelling can be created in paint, or the idea of panelling can simply be expressed by a series of painted lines. Here, blue lines painted onto crusted old whitewash successfully convey the idea of panelling in an eighteenth-century painted room in Sweden. The use of thin lines as well as thick suggests mouldings and the 'field' of the panels.

This kind of ad-hoc decoration can be cheaply and quickly done and requires only a brush, some paint and a steady hand.

LEFT *Early panelling was frequently painted, even though it was generally made of hardwood. Traces of old paint deep in the grain of this sixteenth-century oak panelling show that this was the case here.*

The small scale of the panels, with their plain mouldings, produces a comparatively smooth wall surface. This and the deep frieze (here hung with a damask) are characteristics that were to be revived in the late nineteenth century (see page 100).

frame. This framework, in turn, was fixed to wooden plugs set into the wall. This basic system is common to all successive forms of panelling. Although panelling was broken up by virtue of its construction, these early forms produced a comparatively smooth surface, with little difference in depth between the framing and the panels.

The earliest panelled walls were often painted in floral designs or decorated in trompe l'oeil to look as though the panels were carved or even pyramidal. If polished wood was used the panels were sometimes inlaid with other woods, and in grand schemes, pilasters might separate the sections of panelling, giving a classical rhythm to the wall. Oak was the principal wood used – it was cheap and plentiful and was often worked unseasoned to make it easier to cut.

As the seventeenth century progressed, individual panels became bigger and grew in decorative importance as the newly emerged 'designer' had more influence over the ensemble. Bolection mouldings pushed the surface of the panel forward from the framework, creating a more articulated and richer effect, with light and shadow breaking up the surface of the wall. A variety of woods was used, sometimes painted, sometimes varnished or polished.

RIGHT *A variety of panelling styles can be seen at Pallant House, Sussex. The raised and fielded panels of the area above the chair rail, set in simple quarter-round mouldings, typify the simple classicism of the 1740s, whereas the door architrave and chair rail both have an earlier, Baroque character which is more in tune with the bolection mouldings visible in the further room. No doubt the different characters of these two styles were fully appreciated and deliberately used here.*

The flat surface of the baseboard – but not its moulding – is painted black. This is typical of the period and, apart from being a practical defence against sweeping and mopping, it provides a note of visual strength where wall and floor meet.

Most panelling was painted, although this was not invariably the case. Colours were dark 'wood' shades, such as 'oak-panelling' colour, commonly called 'wainscot', or the other, mostly earth-based colours that one would expect of the period. Because the surface itself was now inherently more modelled, trompe l'oeil effects were not usually employed but marbling and graining, to simulate more exotic materials, began to be used.

By the early eighteenth century, an increase in trade brought imported softwood into Europe, often from northern Russia. Slow-grown trees yielded lumber of immensely superior quality to that which is generally available today. Since it was much easier to work than the traditional oak, larger panels could be cut and mouldings with more complex profiles could be produced.

When Palladianism swept into fashion in England in the early decades of the eighteenth century, panelling was organized to express the classical elements of the wall, in the main cornice, dado and baseboard divisions described on page 62. The cornice especially was often elaborately boxed out but the loss of space which resulted from the use of panelling posed no problems in the large rooms of the period. Sometimes the dado was no longer panelled as such, but was simply planked with wide softwood boards set horizontally to form a smooth surface between chair rail and baseboard. In North America, where wood was the principal building material, the widespread use of panelling was soon established and, with local variations, became a traditional decorative technique.

By the middle of the eighteenth century, the Rococo style, developing from many different strands at the end of the Baroque period, became, in England and its colonies, inextricably mixed with the Palladian style. In Continental Europe, on the other hand, the challenge of fusing the essentially rectilinear construction of panelling with the curvilinear appeal of the Rococo was met by craftsmen at all levels and gave birth to the French form of panelling known as *boiserie*. Here, the surface was smooth, modelling was in low relief, and panel outlines (particularly at their tops) became curved and were carved with elegant, stylized leaves and flowers. Much ingenuity was expended in creating rooms with subtly rounded corners and sensuously finished surfaces.

Indeed, as the century progressed, relief modelling was reduced, not only in the anti-classical Rococo style but also in the newly evolving Neoclassical taste. Though the panels themselves remained large, they tended to be more or less on the same plane as the framework which held them in place, and the framing itself was simpler and more mechanical in

The rectilinear structure of this Louis XV room has almost disappeared beneath the elegant curves of the Rococo panelling. The treatment of the ceiling, which is slightly domed and painted to look like sky, dissolves its hard lines in a similar way. The picking out of the moulding in shades of deep blue emphasizes the shapes of the panels, while a considerable amount of ingenuity has been used to absorb the door catches into the decorative scheme – a central knob outside the room operates a long latch on the inside, which is curved to match the rail of the door.

nature. The panelling was painted, as before, in 'wood' or 'stone' colours, or was grained or marbled.

Where a colour, wallpaper or fabric was used above dado panelling in eighteenth-century rooms, the convention seems to have been to paint the chair rail a neutral and usually pale shade, like the rest of the joinery, and to confine the colour or pattern to the upper part of the wall. This often meant a darker wall than dado. However, if colour was carried over both surfaces it was, when differentiated at all, generally used in a darker shade below the dado.

By the end of the eighteenth century, panelling had become much less important in the decoration of the room, sometimes being no more than a smooth background on which to hang paper or fabric. The difference between the Palladian version and this type of panelling of a couple of generations later can be seen in the way doors changed. They had highly articulated, sculptural panels at the beginning of the century; at the turn of the century, Neoclassical Soane-style doors almost approximate to the modern flush door, with mouldings shrunk to inset beads defining the various parts. This beading had more than a decorative function: the joint where two pieces of wood meet is always prone to opening as the wood swells and shrinks and the bead was a useful device for making this inevitable break seem intentional.

Another tradition of panelling was 'matchboarding' or 'matched boarding' which had begun as boards set between posts. Matchboarding remained a rustic form of wall cladding and changed little over the

Large, plain, unmoulded panels form the bold dado of this early eighteenth-century staircase in a small townhouse. The boards that make up the panels follow the rake of the stairs, and are then set vertically on the landing. The turned balusters, typical of this date (the 1730s), provide the only note of richness in a form of ornamentation that could be produced relatively easily.

centuries, but came into widespread use during the nineteenth century because of the increased ease of producing the boards, with their tongued and grooved edges and characteristic 'v' joints. Almost exclusively of softwood, and painted, matchboarding was applied to the walls and ceilings of farmhouses, inns and public houses. At its simplest, matchboarding is 'v' jointed, though more elaborate forms have a bead dividing the 'v' to help to conceal the joint. As a finish, matchboarding was convenient and practical and had a reputation for being healthy and sanitary – it could be easily cleaned or repainted and hid the fungus and parasites associated with damp walls.

By the middle of the nineteeth century, panelling began to look distinctly old-fashioned and was not common in ordinary domestic interiors. Wooden dados were a practical solution for areas of the house, such as kitchens and hallways, where the wall needed extra protection, but it was only on the very grandest scale, where it still imparted a palatial air, that panelling was used for its decorative qualities – and for its romantic associations.

With the Arts and Crafts movement in the later nineteenth century came a revival of interest in handwork, medieval carving and the rustic

The bedrooms in the house shown opposite have board-lined walls, with narrow battens to cover the joints – something like an early form of the matchboarding that was widely used before the tongued and grooved joint was perfected. The doors of panelled rooms are always treated in a complementary manner to the walls, though not necessarily matching them. Here the door, simply made of narrow boards, has a distinctly handcrafted look. The best decorative treatment for simple, relatively early panelling of this kind is to paint the panelling, doors and window surrounds all alike.

past, all of which meant that rooms became 'woodier'. A version of seventeenth-century oak panelling came into fashion in which the usual proportions were turned upside down, the dado disappeared and the panelling stopped well short of the ceiling, giving room for a deep decorative frieze. The wide ledge where the panelling ended was known as a 'Delft rack' because it was so often used to display Delft china. Fake finishes, such as graining and marbling, were at odds with the ethos of the movement, which eschewed simulation of any description. Wood was exposed for what it was or else, as in the radical 1870s interiors of the English architect Norman Shaw (1831–1912), painted white.

Panelling in Modern Interiors

Frequently used in libraries and studies, panelling is ideal for rooms that can benefit from its organizational quality. It combines well with shelves, as in the traditional library, and can be a very good way of determining the hanging of a collection of pictures. It is not, however, the type of finish one would immediately consider for a bedroom, although the rather old-fashioned look of plain painted panelling has a wonderfully nostalgic feel – such rooms could be spare rooms on half-forgotten corridors in rambling country houses. And in a kitchen, which must accommodate a variety of appliances with different openings, doors, projections and so on, it would clearly not be ideal.

Panelling has not lost its practical advantages. In service areas such as hallways, stairs and bathrooms, it provides a tough surface which can withstand knocks and scrapes and hide a tangle of wires and pipework. Half-panelling up to dado level has always been a means of combining the advantages of a practical surface, on the part of the wall that receives most wear, with more precious materials and finishes, on the upper wall. Different styles of panelling have different proportions. It is important to consider the size of panels in relation to the scale of the room, with smaller panels generally working better in smaller areas.

MATERIALS

If you propose to install panelling, it is important to be environmentally sensitive about which wood you choose, limiting your choice to native species or, if imported, to wood from managed estates. Unfortunately, hardwood is expensive and panelling built by craftsmen is even more so. Softwood panelling is much cheaper and easier to work with. Although ready-to-assemble panels are available in kit form from trade suppliers, it is preferable to avoid their prefabricated look and go back to the traditional methods of construction. Real panelling is jointed so that the wood can expand and contract with variations in humidity; a big panel will absorb a good deal of moisture and move fairly dramatically. Grooves allow the wood play and prevent wide panels, necessarily jointed, from splitting down the middle. A good construction guide is, of course, invaluable if you propose to make the panelling yourself; the correct mouldings can be spindled very cheaply. The process is complex and requires considerable skill, but it is not much more expensive than faking panelling with ready-made mouldings and medium-density

Towards the end of the nineteenth century, pre-classical forms were enthusiastically revived by the Arts and Crafts movement. Small panels, a deep frieze and built-in oak dressers are combined with the more classical proportions of a shuttered Georgian sash window to produce this revolutionary Arts and Crafts room designed by Philip Webb. The softwood panelling is painted an artistic (but sensible) dark blue-green, while the oak elements are polished. Blue and white Delft or Chinese china, never out of fashion, was especially popular for Arts and Crafts interiors, and the shelf above the panelling provided a perfect place for displaying it.

fibreboard (MDF). This fabricated sheet material is useful and exceptionally stable and uniform but does not age or behave like a natural material. Plywood, on the other hand, is available with facings of different woods, including birch and ash. It takes a stainer and polish very well and retains a grainy appearance even when painted. While pine can be used, its orange shade is not always acceptable – and, in any case, historical precedent calls for it to be painted.

Surface Treatments

Hardwood panelling is usually not painted but left to display its beauty as naturally as possible, finished in a simple way with either waxing or French polishing.

Softwood panelling has always been painted, as softwood has never been considered as anything other than a building material: only in the last few decades has pine been stripped and exposed. In the 1920s and '30s, many historic rooms in museums on both sides of the Atlantic were stripped to reveal details of construction and carving. At the same time, fashionable decorators such as Syrie Maugham (1879–1955) created a vogue for 'pickled' (limed) or artificially lightened wood.

Paint, of course, covers the wood entirely. Latex is not suitable, and instead oil paint must be used – either gloss, eggshell or flat (matt), depending on the intended finish. Flat finish is generally considered best, especially for the paler colours, but as it is not very hardwearing, eggshell is often used instead. Panelling that is painted in dark and rich colours or that is dimly lit often benefits from some degree of surface shine – gloss paint can be used to achieve this.

RIGHT *The panelling here is entirely new and was made from two thicknesses of medium density fibreboard and specially spindled mouldings. The room is organized by a system of wide and narrow panels, stopped deliberately short to accommodate the original cornice. The chimney piece – also new – was marbled in black with yellow and pale grey markings. The 'Chineseness' of the wall colour is emphasized by the design of the curtain fabric and the pagoda shape of the pelmet.*

The detail (LEFT) shows my painting scheme for the panels, stiles and rails. The stippled panel was painted first and the moulding was then dragged in the same colour as the stippling and wiped to lighten it. The stiles and rails, dragged in a darker tone, were painted last, as described on page 121. The yellow glaze used in this scheme is made of roughly equal parts of white flat oil and glazing liquid, coloured with artists' oil paints and thinned out almost to wateriness with turpentine. The colours used were cadmium yellow and golden ochre over a base coat of cool cream.

BLEACHING, LIMING AND STAINING

The basic colour of wood can be lightened by liming, to retain the essential 'woodiness' of a panelled room while making it appear less dark. For an even lighter tone, a special bleach for wood is available from trade suppliers. Staining completely changes the colour of wood, especially if it is bleached first.

Bleaching

Bleaching takes the colour out of wood, to make it more or less white. Use proprietary woodbleach and follow the safety advice and instructions on the pack carefully. Bleached wood may be stained or limed or simply varnished or wax polished.

Liming

Liming developed as a treatment for oak and other open-grained hardwoods, but other woods can also be limed. Traditionally, oak is darkened first, but undarkened or bleached wood can be given the same treatment. Softwood may be sealed with shellac first to make it less absorbent.

To darken oak for liming, brush or swab it with ammonia (which creates dangerous fumes, so wear a mask and rubber gloves and work in a well-ventilated room). This method is better than applying a stain or pigment.

Before liming, wood is usually brushed in the direction of the grain with a coarse wire brush to open up the grain. The liming is executed by rubbing or brushing on, then lightly wiping off, a white pigment, which may be distemper, paint, filler or home-made or proprietary liming wax. Wax is probably the easiest, and can be polished when dry. Softwoods, because of their absorbency, and beech, because of the nature of its grain, are best limed with a very thin white paint, applied by brush. Painted liming can be sealed with shellac, waxed or varnished.

Staining

Wood that is to be stained must first be bleached, especially where stain colours would be distorted by the yellow, red or brown tones of the natural wood. Blue, green and pure yellow, in particular, need a bleached backing. When dry, stained wood is usually sealed with wax or varnish to protect it (unless the stain is varnish-based).

Wood stains are available in spirit-, oil-, or water-based forms. You can also make your own stains by tinting varnish or polish with stainers or artists' paints. Tinted varnishes, carefully applied, can provide wonderfully deep and lustrous colours, and are on the way to becoming lacquer. Several coats, each carefully rubbed down to remove the rough 'nibs' (flecks of dust in the varnish) give an exceptionally rich, smooth finish.

If varnish is used to seal the stained wood, two coats of eggshell varnish should be applied. Tinted varnish will make the wood appear darker.

The samples illustrated below show a length of plain oak that has been treated in a variety of ways. From left to right: plain and untreated, bleached, stained (after being bleached), darkened with ammonia, limed (after being darkened), varnished.

RIGHT *Liming can be a successful treatment for modern interiors as well as for period rooms. In this house in Barbados, wood that has been bleached and limed to look like driftwood is combined with dry, unpolished stone walls and a polished granite floor to evoke the seashore.*

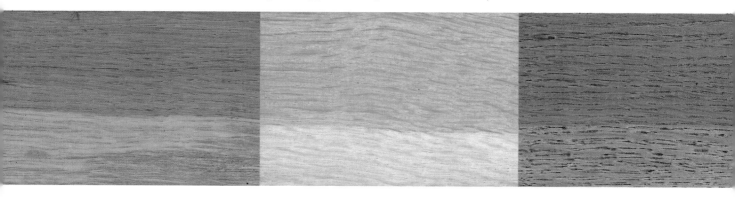

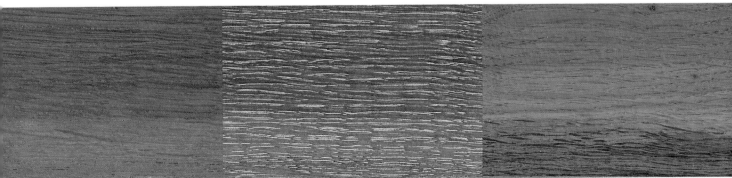

GRAINING

Whatever medium it is worked in, graining is essentially a darker, translucent coat applied over a paler, solid undercoat. Then, using a combination of additive and subtractive techniques – brushing on and taking off – separately or together, the wet top coat is broken up and 'arranged' in a pattern to resemble the grain of wood. Up to two or three graining coats can be applied, in different tones or different colours, and fine details added for verisimilitude. Alternatively, the finish can be more overtly decorative: the traditional North American technique, using vinegar or beer as the medium, results in such a finish, with alternately thick and thin patches lifted off. For credibility, follow the grain of the wood when graining; on panels, this can be assumed to run from top to bottom unless the panels are of 'landscape' shape, in which case the grain will run horizontally.

Mahogany

Mahogany graining (RIGHT, ABOVE) in a free and flamboyant manner that owes much to eighteenth-century work. This is very different from the elaborately 'realistic' work of the later nineteenth century.

This type of work has to be done quickly. The sample was worked in gouache thinned with beer, on a red ground painted in a ready-mixed paint (the strip on the left of the sample). The gouache colours used were burnt umber and black.

1 Brush on the graining colour so that it is evenly coated. Make sure that the colour has got everywhere. Then use a whisk broom to drag the length of the panel with a slight sweep, followed by a second, lighter drag with a slightly different sweep which will blur the hard edges a little.

2 With a badger softener or a soft dusting brush, rapidly and very lightly work across the grain as shown on the right-hand side of the panel.

RIGHT *Burr or burl veneers have always been sought after for furniture. They are cut from the rooty part of a tree or from the monstrous growths that occasionally form. Here a door has been skilfully painted to harmonize with the dado. Its unusual patterns of twisted grain, knots and almost marble-like markings are typical of burr wood. The grainer turns and twists the brush, adds knots with the fingertips and softens and mottles in circular patterns.*

Oak

Oak graining is lighter in colour than mahogany and is flecked to suggest the grain. This sample (LEFT, BELOW) was also worked in beer mixed with gouache – using yellow ochre and raw umber with a little white, on a dark cream ground.

1 Proceed as in step **1** for mahogany. To simulate the rather coarse, 'woven' texture of oak in a calligraphic and impressionistic manner, the first two brushings should leave the markings more or less like the left-hand side of the sample.

2 Then draw a steel comb (if new, with its teeth well smoothed on a fine stone or emery cloth) diagonally through the still wet graining colour to break the streaks into dashes. The effect is shown on the right-hand side of the panel.

At this point the nineteenth-century grainer would have used a small horn or tortoiseshell blade or a penny wrapped in cloth to 'wipe out' the characteristic figuring of oak. Such a pattern can be very distracting, however, and is usually best avoided.

DRAGGING

The technique of dragging, revived within the last twenty years or so and employed as a wall finish, was first used on timber, and specifically on panelling and doors. It developed from 'flatting', a method employed by craftsmen-painters in the eighteenth and nineteenth centuries. They were often called upon to 'flat' the surface with a final coat consisting of a thin mixture of pigment and turpentine with very little or no oil, thus producing an attractive matt surface. At the same time, the flatting coat provided an opportunity subtly to alter the colour, sharpening or dulling it. Because of its composition, which lacked the strength (and therefore also the shine) of oil, the flatting coat was always very fragile but, like many fragile finishes, it has a subtle beauty and as it ages, so long as it is not abused, it gradually acquires that distinctive and alluring patina characteristic of old paintwork. Dragging uses paint glazes to produce similar effects.

While the dragging technique with which we are familiar today really originated in flatting, it is in turn related to graining. Like graining, it

This recently painted eighteenth-century panelling has been strongly dragged and quite boldly picked out. I dragged the panels first, in the direction of the grain, then the panel mouldings, followed by the stiles and rails and finally the dado moulding. The dragging was done over white eggshell. The colours used to mix the strong red glaze were universal stainers in burnt sienna and red with a very little flat white oil to add opacity. For the mouldings a little of this colour was added to white.

The bolection mouldings of this panelled dining room are typical of their date (c.1710). Scrapes taken from the paintwork revealed that the wood had originally been grained in a rather wild and Baroque version of walnut. The intention here was to create something of the same feeling of movement through marbling in two shades of grey, combined with plain dragged stiles and rails. I painted this decoration in thinned flat paint (using no glazing liquid) over white. On the cornice and mouldings the grey was blended into the still wet flat white, whereas on the panels, stiles and rails the translucency of the thinned paint was exploited by applying it over the dry white paint. The fireplace is marbled in the same manner as the walls, but in black with grey veins.

can be either subtle or brash, unlike graining it has little to do with an attempt to reproduce a natural finish, but instead exploits the decorative association of brushstrokes and wood grain for its own sake, as well as making the most of the translucency of glazed colour. If the contrast between the underlying colour and the dragged layer is great, the effect can be quite insistent and is best restricted to relatively small areas such as mouldings. In more subtle combinations – for example, blue over grey – it can be applied over a wider area. The difficult part of dragging is the beginning and end of each stroke and these areas need to be tidied up with a small brush while the glaze is still workable, to give an even effect. With panelling, it may be neater to stipple the panel itself and reserve the dragging for the mouldings, stiles and rails.

MARBLING

Because real marble cannot be worked in the way that wood can, the use of marbling to decorate panelling is, and always has been, like graining, playful. There is no disguising the fact that the surface is wood – the material remains obvious and is intended to be so. The style of marbling adopted in this context is painterly, making no attempt at realism or trompe l'oeil, and the room remains a panelled and painted one rather than a stony one.

Marbling for panelling is most often carried out in various shades of grey. Different parts can be marbled to look as if they are separate pieces of marble, or even different types of marble; alternatively, the entire wall can be treated as one continuous surface.

ABOVE *Detail of an elaborate plaster cornice high above a grand staircase, tip gilded so that the effect from below is that of a sparkling surface. Tip gilding is relatively economical, both in the time taken in execution and in gold leaf, and it creates a much lighter effect than solid gold.*

In this form of gilding, oil size is brushed on very fast, and then gold leaf is applied to the size when it is almost dry.

RIGHT *This newly decorated room in an important early eighteenth-century Baroque house shows the effect of picking out. The apricot colour, which is very much of our century, has been confined to the panels, stiles and rails, while everything else is treated in whites. The effect is to link the elements of cornice, mouldings, fireplace, doors and baseboards. The door shows the classic way of picking out, using three shades of white dragged over white.*

PICKING OUT

Picking out consists of painting specific areas – usually mouldings or ornament – of an architecturally conceived decorative scheme in different colours or shades. The aim is to distinguish one section from another in places where the architectural features are worthy of emphasis. In the case of panelling, it is of course possible to paint everything in one continuous colour and tone, but for decorative effect, and to emphasize the fact that it *is* panelling, very often it is effective to use different tones for different areas. In this way the structure is emphasized and the scheme acquires dignity and strength.

Picking out can also serve to improve a muddled decorative 'language' by emphasizing its finest characteristics and giving it shape. At its best, the technique can enliven a room; at its worst, it can look pretentious, unnecessary, even ridiculous. A seductive treatment, if overdone it can fragment a surface or room instead of unifying it. And it should never be used to give a room an unwarranted distinction.

There are three main ways of picking out: in tone, in colour or in gold (exceptionally in silver). Picking out using tones of the same colour is the classical approach, much favoured by John Fowler (1906–77) and other twentieth-century decorators. This type of picking out is most often seen in stony, white or neutral colours. Infinitely subtle, it can strengthen and 'explain' a scheme almost invisibly, by deepening shadows and lightening highlights. Conversely, an unbalanced set of tones will distort a scheme and emphasize faults in design.

Colour can also be an effective way of picking out. A contrasting colour is chosen to accentuate detail in small quantities. The colour should be of a different intensity to the surroundings or the spark will be lost: in olive panelling with an orange moulding, for example, the orange accentuates the inherent greenness of the olive colour.

Gilding, or picking out in gold, gives the richest result. Usually reserved for objects, such as frames, it has always been costly and special. It was used in picking out, if at all, in the same way as a contrasting colour might be. True gilding – not the use of gold paint – is almost as complex and multi-faceted a subject as paint. It ranges from the brightest burnished watergilding, which is so reflective as almost to dematerialize the surface, to the dullest metallic bronze.

The most easily available and most reliable finish is oil gilding in pure gold leaf (in various colours), either 'left bright' or 'glazed to dull'. Gilding was extremely effective in the low candle or oil lighting of the eighteenth century and has a similar impact in a darkish room with small pockets of brilliance. Because of the cost of the leaf, it is usually applied in small quantities and often as 'tip gilding', which is an outlining and highlighting finish on carved and moulded ornament. This practice was a nineteenth-century refinement; in the eighteenth century, leaf was used solid, emphasizing the sculptural mass rather than linearity and surface.

Refinement in Baroque gilding was achieved more by varying the colour and lustre of the gold from place to place, alternating burnished with matt or even 'sanded' areas. For a sanded surface, sand was sprinkled on before sizing to give a rough, broken finish full of points of maximum light and dark.

Faking Panelling

From an early point in its decorative history, almost from its first appearance in the sixteenth century, wood panelling has been simulated in a variety of ways, using a range of different materials. Imitation was sometimes simply a question of borrowing the decorative language of panelling and applying it to a new medium. A very early form of faked panelling was Pompeiian wall decoration, rediscovered towards the end of the eighteenth century. Throughout the Middle Ages, walls in churches were enriched with painted panels, sometimes unadorned, sometimes framing biblical scenes. Fake panelling was economical and easy to execute and, like real panelling, was a way of dividing large surfaces into more convenient and approachable sections. Early in the eighteenth century when plaster began to come into widespread and general use, it was moulded *in situ* into panels which copied the articulation of wood panelling. Later on, the same effect could be gained by using ready-made plaster mouldings. Such prefabrication was one of the essentials of the Adams' approach to design, and parallel developments in manufacturing industries in the later eighteenth century were not coincidental.

Paint was also an easy means of simulating panelling. At the very simplest, almost abstract, level this could take the form of lines painted on the wall, dividing the surface in the same manner as panelling. This type of effect can be seen in the rooms of eighteenth-century Scandinavia, where brightly coloured lines, often in shades of blue, were

LEFT *Faked and real panelling have been combined in this mid-eighteenth-century room, which accommodates wardrobes behind the panelled doors and drawers in the dado. Moulding has been applied to the wall surface over the mantelpiece and round the room to fake matching panels. The old mantelpiece itself was rescued from a demolition site and has been given 'slips' of old Delft tiles.*

RIGHT *Painted lines and bands of colour make no pretence at creating a third dimension in this rich little room in Sweden. The intriguing hollow corner forms the centre of the spiral staircase – whose underside is enriched with wonderful arabesques. This is faked panelling reduced to its decorative and abstract minimum.*

RIGHT *The close-up detail in a French-style painted room shows very clearly the grand fluted pilaster at the corner of a Neoclassical panel. The grain of the plaster is seen through the controlled paintwork and the effect is formal and elegant.*

LEFT *Beautifully modulated tones of subdued pale blue organized into simple trompe l'oeil panelling make of an undistinguished room something very special. The dry-looking paintwork of the walls – in two shades, with highlights and shadows – matches the Ikat curtains, restrained by cloakpins, to perfection.*

applied over whitewash. Similarly, Pompeiian decoration, revived in the early years of the nineteenth century, was carried out in paint, with wide and narrow margins echoing the antique precedent.

Later in the nineteenth century, very elaborate trompe l'oeil panelled effects, including highly realistic versions of graining, were executed in paint with great skill. By the middle of the century, wallpaper was available printed to look like panelling, making it possible to buy a panelled room by the roll.

In this century, taking the idea of trompe panelling to its most extreme degree, painters like Rex Whistler have created entire painted rooms which simulate not only panelling but also the inset paintings, tapestry or lacquerwork that panelling was so often used to display.

PANELS IN PAINT

Much simulated panelling, today as in the past, is carried out in paint. The approach can be purely decorative, dividing the wall into rectangular sections as a reminder of panelling, or it can be illusionist to a greater or lesser degree.

In the decorative sense, painting lines on the wall in the configurations of panelling does not suggest any change of depth, but instead is a way of introducing a colour for its own sake. The vivid blue bands in Scandinavian interiors form just such a use of colour as accent, adding a certain crispness and graphic emphasis to the rooms. Painting mouldings in a sharp contrasting shade has much the same effect.

LEFT *This tall drawing room retains its delicate plaster ceiling and a cornice but no other original features. In the decorative scheme I devised for the room, the first step was to 'lower' the ceiling by introducing a strong frieze and a dado. The remaining wall surface was then 'flip-flapped' twice in very thin latex tinted with raw and burnt sienna, and, to model the wall, shallow inset panels were suggested by dark and light lines.*

The ornamented ceiling was strengthened with colour, to bring it down further. The designs of the frieze and the ornaments for the narrower panels come from a book of 1777–92 by Michelangelo Pergolesi. These were stencilled in white and given freehand shadows.

It was important not to over-enrich the walls – which would then have advanced, squeezing the ceiling, that had been so carefully brought down, back up again.

Painted panelling naturally offers a freedom not available when dealing with real wood. Even so, for any simulation to be effective the work must be planned in advance. At the outset, make sure that the proposed wall divisions follow a logic of their own. You might like to alternate narrower panels with wider ones, using the narrow ones for siting wall lights and the wider panels for hanging pictures. Take into account how windows or doors will affect the composition and measure carefully so that unequal margins are not left at either side. Choose a style of 'panelling' which will be in keeping with its setting.

In general, the simpler your aims the more convincing the final effect will be. At the most basic level of illusion, simple dragging or brush-graining techniques can be used to give the feel of a wood surface, organized in the predetermined panelling arrangement. Conventionally, the stiles and rails are always darker than the panels, whereas mouldings are lighter than the panels. Even a slight difference between the tones will help to suggest articulation.

For full-blown trompe l'oeil, it is necessary to consider the effect of light, principally the effect of natural light. This is because the illusory effect rests on the placing of shadows and highlights to give the work a three-dimensional quality. It is obviously important that the shadows should be consistent across the wall, not jumbled up as if the light were coming in different directions at once. It is usually best to follow the main source of light and ignore artificial sources. The eye also finds it hard to accept elements which appear to be recessed from the picture plane while at the same time other elements seem to be (or really are) advancing. For this reason, it can be difficult, for instance, successfully to mix trompe l'oeil panelling with a projecting dado.

RIGHT *The door at the end of this little passage that connects three rooms has been made of coreboard. I painted it in trompe l'oeil to look like a six-panelled mahogany door with raised and fielded panels copying the style of the original eighteenth-century doors of the neighbouring rooms (not visible in the photograph). The walls are painted to look as though they are of stone blocks and the little columns are marbled. The floor is of Westmorland slate, inlaid in geometric patterns.*

In preparing these fake-panelled dados I first worked out the sizes of the panels and drew them in pencil. The simple panels (ABOVE LEFT) were painted as described in detail on pages *120–1*, using off-white paint glazes.

A slightly more complicated painted dado (ABOVE RIGHT) simulates raised and fielded panels. Here the surface of the 'panel' has been spattered, with everything else masked off – not so much to make it resemble granite as to introduce colour. Then off-white 'shadows' and 'highlights' have been treated in much the same way as in the simple panelling, except that here there are bead mouldings and a painted 'shadow' below the real chair rail.

The off-whites were mixed from white and raw umber with a little yellow ochre and black. The paint was then 'opened up' with about $\frac{1}{3}$ of glazing liquid before being thinned as much as needed. Arriving at the right consistency is a matter for trial and error. The degree of thinness required varies, depending on the speed of working, the effect wanted, the size of the panels, the type of brush used, the temperature of the room and whether there is a passage of air over the surface. The right consistency will be found to work easily.

RIGHT This small bedroom has been given painted fake panelling. Because the surface of the wall was not in particularly good condition, the painting was done rather boldly and the style of 'panelling' chosen was accordingly simple – an unmoulded version of an early eighteenth-century style, with baseboard, chair and cornice 'rails' separating the 'panels' horizontally and with vertical divisions, in the same colour, representing the stiles. Step-by-step details for the painting are given on pages *120–1*.

A

B

C

PAINTING SIMPLE TROMPE L'OEIL PANELS

The style of faked panelling you choose should be in keeping with the room and its details, and the layout can be used to disguise any displeasing proportions or features, such as awkwardly positioned windows and doors. Planning the design and layout of the panelling therefore needs careful thought before you begin.

In working out a design, the type of panelling on the doors (and shutters, if there are any) may help to dictate a style for the faked panels themselves. The position of the fireplace and windows must be taken into account so that the panelling fits well around them. Panels can also be designed to suit the placing of dominant pieces of furniture.

In this small bedroom, illustrated on page 119, the section of wall between the window and the corner of the room dictated the size of the narrowest 'panel'. A 'panel' of the same size was then repeated on the other side of the window to give symmetry and the same narrow 'panels' were used to flank the fireplace, positioned across a corner of the room. The remaining wall spaces were regularly divided, except for a 'panel' behind the bed, which was designed to be the same width as the bed. Finally, the way natural light fell from the window dictated the placing of highlights and shadows.

The basic colour in the scheme illustrated here is a light pinky orange, slightly reminiscent of cedar wood. The 'panel' colour is paler and pinker than that for the 'stiles' and 'rails'. To make highlights where real moulding would catch the light from the window, a little of the panel colour was added to white; for shadows, burnt umber was added to the 'stiles' and 'rails' colour. The walls were first prepared and painted with white eggshell to make them as smooth as possible. The paint for the panelling was a paint glaze made from half and half flat oil and glazing liquid tinted with stainers in two shades.

1 When the base coat is dry pencil in the 'panel' shapes, following your design, and using a straight edge and spirit level (A).

2 Make the paint glaze for the 'panels' and brush lightly onto the surface using a wide brush (10cm/4in). Then drag an almost dry brush from top to bottom in long strokes, keeping side edges as neat as possible. Allow the strokes to overrun the pencil lines at top and bottom to avoid an obvious stopping mark (B).

3 Tidy up the edges of the panels using a cloth or paper towel soaked in turpentine (C). Keep a steady hand and change the rag when saturated. Allow to dry.

4 Mix the darker glaze for the 'stiles' and 'rails'. Brush on in a thin layer and drag as before. The order (and consequent overlapping) in which these elements are painted helps to create the illusion of construction.

Paint the intermediate verticals first, interrupting them at the chair rail. Then add the horizontal elements – cornice, chair and baseboard 'rails' – which should be continuous, but should stop short at the corners. Finally add the corner verticals, working right from the top to the bottom. Allow to dry thoroughly.

5 The final stage is to add shadows and highlights, using a straight edge, No. 3 sable brush and the appropriate colour – and keeping a steady hand! The order of execution is unimportant.

For shadows (D), paint a narrow line 1cm/½in wide, either entirely on the 'panel' or slightly overlapping onto the 'rail' (which helps to tidy any wobbly edges). Highlights (E) are painted in exactly the same way. The corners where highlights and shadow lines meet should be mitred. The natural source of light should determine where your shadows and highlights fall. Here (F), the window is on the right and throws light onto the left-hand and bottom edges of each 'panel', while shadows are cast on the right-hand and top edges.

PAPER PANELS

Simulated panelling can be achieved in paper, adopting one of three approaches. First, panelling can be simulated by applying trompe paper borders to the wall. These are printed to resemble carved mouldings. Alternatively, to suggest an abstract notion of panelling, it is possible to stick on strips of plain coloured paper to form rectangular shapes. Finally, paper can be used more decoratively, with borders suggesting the rhythm of panels.

In the nineteenth century, entire rooms might be papered in grained paper, the first 'wood effect' design. The room would subsequently be varnished to intensify the effect. Many other types of paper imitating wood finishes and patterns are available today.

USING MOULDINGS

Panelling can be simulated three-dimensionally by applying wooden or plaster mouldings to break up the wall in the required pattern.

The French eighteenth-century style of panelling is perhaps best suited to this stick-on approach. The *boiserie* room of the eighteenth century, with its curvilinear moulding and Rococo ornament, relies very little on architectural or three-dimensional modelling in the sense that the Palladian room does. Today, hardware stores sell wooden mouldings, corners, crestings, and so on, which can be assembled to make charming Rococo panelled rooms. The finish – the colours and the quality of the glazing and gilding – is, of course, what counts.

There is a wide variety of ready-made mouldings available from hardware stores and lumberyards. It may also be possible to have mouldings made to a specific profile. Choose a suitable style of moulding to create the desired effect. For a hint of French *boiserie*, for example, as in the room shown opposite, combine gently arching mouldings with straight sections.

1 When using mouldings, first work out the arrangement of the panels on paper. Draw the shapes on the wall. Then cut the mouldings to length, using a mitre box for the corners. Hold them in position to make sure they are the correct length before fixing them in place.

2 If the wall surface is absolutely flat, adhesive may be all that is required for fixing, but generally wire brads – fine, headless nails – will be needed as well. An adhesive combined with filler (making it bulkier than ordinary glue) creates a tight seal. Smooth any excess filler with the fingers, fill edges, corners or nail holes and apply undercoat to the mouldings and wall.

3 The three-dimensional quality of the mouldings can be accentuated by adding painted shadows and highlights, or the mouldings can be painted as part of the decorative scheme. By tradition, mouldings are painted in a lighter shade than the panels or in a contrasting colour.

RIGHT *For this French-style panelling, three shades of French grey were used to paint 2.5cm/1in bands within the central panels to give them visual importance. The lightest shade was used for the surrounds and the middle of the central panels. This particular shade of grey can be created by adding Payne's grey and Indian red to white.*

THE ORIENTAL ROOM

Decorative interpretations of oriental themes and motifs are many and varied. This elegant interior conveys the essence of the Oriental Room, with its delicately patterned wallpaper, its Chinese yellow tones and lacquered fake bamboo furniture. Gothick and chinoiserie, for their extravagance and unfamiliarity, were often fused in decorative schemes. This thirteenth-century (genuine Gothic) 'birdcage' room is just such a hybrid – papered with a Chinese bird paper, the extra details created in paint are Gothick and Rococo. Cut-out paper birds have been added to the vaulting and honey-coloured Chinese straw matting has been fitted to the floor.

A fascination with the Orient is deeply rooted in Western culture. Exotic, enticing, endlessly mysterious, the East has provided a continuing strand in decorating that is typified by particular colours, motifs and materials. Many of the elements of the Oriental Room can be traced back to objects that were imported into Europe from the Far East at the beginning of trade between East and West in the late Middle Ages; others owe more to imaginative licence and reinterpretation.

One European tempted by the lure of Cathay was the Venetian traveller Marco Polo (1254–1324) who followed his father on trading expeditions to Peking and entered the service of the Mongol emperor Kublai Khan. To reach the Far East, Marco Polo used the old Silk Road, an overland route established in antiquity as a trading link enabling Chinese silk to be exchanged for precious metals from the Mediterranean. This tenuous link, never severed completely, was used only rarely in later years.

Marco Polo's accounts of his travels, alongside the limited number of textiles, carpets and pieces of porcelain that arrived in the West at this time, created an impression of unbelievable exoticism in the Western imagination – an impression which was reinforced and elaborated by other, more fictitious, travellers' tales. In the fourteenth century, the popular *Voiage of Sir John Manndevile*, which purported to be by the traveller himself but which was actually a French work compiled from a number of different sources, mixed fact and fiction in a fantastical way. Describing a voyage to the South Pole, for instance, the 'author' claimed that it became so cold that words froze in the air and fell to the deck of the ship, only to thaw and be heard as jumbled nonsense as they regained warmer waters. In the context of these tales, which largely concentrated on the strange customs and creatures that were said to originate in the Far and Near East, it is not surprising that the few oriental artefacts that did reach Europe during this period were prized as magical objects. Porcelain, in particular, was thought to have special powers that made it proof against poison.

It was not until the European expansionism of the seventeenth century – when the globe began to be more confidently, and accurately, mapped – that trade became more efficiently organized. The empire building of the English, Dutch and Portuguese and the new sea routes

they established around Africa increased the volume of trade from a trickle to a flood. Because so much traffic passed through India en route to and from China and Japan, 'India', as represented most forcefully in the European mind by the exploits of the British-owned East India Company (incorporated in 1600), became synonymous with the Far East or the exotic, the embodiment of Cathay. At this time, trade still consisted of authentic goods made in China for the Chinese.

Western Interpretations of the Orient

Towards the end of the seventeenth century, a growing demand for Eastern products and the increasingly sophisticated nature of trade meant that Western merchants and trading companies were able to commission specially designed products for the Western market. This marked the beginning of the hybridization of original Chinese or Far Eastern designs and Western interpretations and, conversely, the oriental reinterpretation of European ideas.

A case in point is the evolution of chintz. Painted and printed cotton or calico had been imported from India since the sixteenth century; 'chintz', as the fabric was termed, became increasingly popular. By the seventeenth century, European adaptations were made to the traditional Indian 'Tree of Life' designs and sent out to India to be produced to order. The finished products, often used as bedcovers or bedhangings, were known as *palampores*. Chintz became so successful, both as a dress fabric and in furnishing, that laws were passed in England to protect the native silk and wool industries. From 1722 chintz could be neither imported nor manufactured; the ban on manufacture was lifted towards the end of the century.

At the same time as European traders were beginning to influence what was produced in the East, Western potteries and furniture-makers started to copy oriental designs for the home market. Lacquered furniture was produced in Western shapes and forms but with Eastern motifs and finishes. The 1688 manual by Stalker and Parker, *A Treatise of Japanning and Varnishing*, instructed painters on the correct techniques for japanning and varnishing and included engravings of oriental designs to be copied onto cabinet fronts, comb and other boxes, looking-glass frames and so on. All the techniques and designs are now clearly seen to be of their time and place but then, no doubt, were considered exotic and mysterious and could initiate the amateur and professional alike into arcane arts – indeed, the amateur in particular is addressed. Japan, moreover, the home of lacquer, had virtually closed itself off from trade with the West. Among Stalker's and Parker's many recipes, advice on buying brushes and engravings of motifs, lies the germ of all that we still today think of as 'oriental'. The willow pattern plate was born here.

The design of the plate is loosely based on certain Chinese ceramics – even though it is entirely European, not to say English. Produced in enormous quantities, in slightly different designs over – so far – two centuries, it is probably hardly noticed as being anything other than a plate (or 'china'). Behind its anonymous near-invisibility lies the whole

LEFT *A simple early panelled room (c. 1700) has been made exotic by superimposing lacquer screens on the plain panelling. Oriental porcelain – ranged on a set of corner shelves, whose outline is reminiscent of a pagoda – adds to the sense of fascination that the East held for the late-seventeenth-century Western world.*

BELOW *This open chintz design, painted in gouache on glazed cotton, was based on a late-eighteenth-century Chinese hand-painted silk. The wide palette of colours was chosen to relate to an old Chinese wallpaper hanging in the same room and combines indigo blue and madder red with other naturalistic colours and with the greens typical of the Chinese painted foliage.*

history of the Western attitude to the East. Blue and white china is at one and the same time so Eastern and so completely ordinary that it can almost be discounted from the point of view of colour in any scheme. Anonymous and invisible as a plate perhaps, the design can – when transformed by a complete change of scale into a scheme for an entire room – become a strong and eccentric feature. The lack of perspective, the apparent conflicts in relative size and scale and the legend of love and brutality depicted on the plates encapsulate the willow vision.

The same is true of Dutch Delft, which began as an attempt to reproduce the look of porcelain but which today has a quite different resonance. The craze for porcelain was spurred by the fashion for tea-drinking, a habit that was rapidly taken up throughout Europe in the late seventeenth century. The indivisibility of the two is neatly illustrated by the fact that cargoes of porcelain were often shipped from China and packed with tea, for safety, in lacquered tea chests.

By the beginning of the eighteenth century, chinoiserie was well established. The asymmetrical nature of much Chinese art had a powerful influence on textile design. Popular silk patterns of this period featured disjointed or jagged backgrounds and almost tropical floral and foliage motifs, an exotic contrast to the stately and well-organized patterns more typical of the Baroque. James Leman (1688–1745), a Huguenot silk designer working in Spitalfields, was one of the leading exponents of such 'Bizarre' silks, as these patterns, popular for a brief period around 1710 throughout Europe, were termed.

Within this asymmetry, the stage was set for the arrival of the Rococo in the second quarter of the eighteenth century, roughly at the same time as Palladianism began to exert its influence on design in England. The Rococo, always more popular in Germany and France than in England, was at variance with the sobriety and order promulgated by the Palladians. It took oriental elements, notably a characteristic asymmetry, as well as more specific motifs and details, and merged these with a light, flowing, decorative line, full of feathery curves and subtle surface embellishment. Porcelain was an important means of expressing the new style and the factory at Meissen in Germany, established in 1710, was soon able to produce delicately coloured and exquisitely modelled wares, arguably the height of artistic achievement in that medium.

The brief flowering of the Rococo in England, where it touched all aspects of artistic endeavour, was in part the manifestation of a desire to return to a more natural look. The elaborate symmetries of the Baroque were deliberately cast aside and an equally – to modern eyes at any rate – artificial style of light, asymmetrical, playful and deliberately outlandish forms was invented. This was both French and oriental, the 'foreignness' of both influences being vital to the concept.

The elements of the style, as it affected Northern Europe and therefore also North America, were a delight in asymmetry; the use of 'c' and 's' scrolls, abstract curves terminating in scrolls that are the essence of the Chippendale style; an emphasis on the countryside – birds, beasts, flowers and milkmaids – and a fair dash of chinoiserie in the form, inevitably, of pagodas, hoo-hoo birds, a dragon or two and some fantastical plants.

ABOVE *Oriental motifs from ceramics and textiles decorate a small modern mirror frame. I painted the green details on a cream ground to recall the furniture made by Chippendale for the eighteenth-century actor and dramatist David Garrick. Cleaning has recently revealed that Garrick's furniture was actually blue and white – the colour of porcelain – rather than the green and cream (caused by a coat of yellowed varnish) which I copied.*

LEFT *Details from Chinese wallpapers and oriental ceramics are combined with wild Rococo marbling to create a porcelain room in Tureholm. Sweden was a considerable importer of China wares and has a strong tradition of decorative painting. This naïve interpretation is truly fantastic. The monochrome palette is not the least part of its charm.*

LEFT *Throughout the eighteenth century, Chinese workshops produced an enormous range of goods in huge quantities for the Western market. A typical wallpaper design might consist of flowering trees, with small plants at ground level and exotic birds or butterflies decorating the branches. Equally popular for their glimpses of oriental life were papers such as this one at Winterthur in the United States. Here there is no attempt to suggest real depth and distance – as in a conventional mural landscape – and (to modern eyes) the quirky perspective and subtle colouring ensure that the walls of the room retain their integrity. The characteristic dark paintwork is a perfect foil for the Chinese export porcelain. The chairs, in a Chippendale design, incorporate Gothick and Chinese details.*

Although Palladianism and the Rococo appear to be diametrically opposed, Chinese wallpaper was one point at which they intersected. In England especially, Chinese papers were often put up in classical, Palladian rooms, applied above dado-panelling, or were used as a substitute for silk damask wallcoverings. There was no pretence at creating a Chinese room – certainly not as it would have been recognized by a native of China.

Painted papers had been imported from the East since the middle of the seventeenth century. Soon, as in other areas, the preferences of European merchants had an effect on the designs, and the needs of the 'industry' standardized some aspects. Chinese papers were usually hand painted, although the outlines of some were printed from enormous blocks. They were produced in standard widths of about 1.2m/4ft and sold in sets. When a set of panels was hung, the joints were often disguised by adding branches, birds or butterflies cut from spare pieces of paper.

By the middle of the eighteenth century, the Rococo style, which in its late form reached the limits of elaboration, was on the wane, to be superseded by Neoclassicism. With the eclipse of the Rococo went chinoiserie, and an equivalent interest in things oriental did not recur until the end of the century. When the oriental influence returned, it did

RIGHT *A dressing room in the Court Theatre at Drottningholm, Sweden, is decorated, in chinoiserie style, with a hand-painted Swedish imitation of Chinese paper. Boldly painted, with calligraphic flourishes and in a limited palette, the charm of this paper results partly from its naivety and partly from its scale. The dressing rooms at Drottningholm are notoriously small, this design is quite large and its details scaled up. The 'doll's house' simplicity that results is reinforced by the incongruity of the bare scrubbed boards and Rococo gilt.*

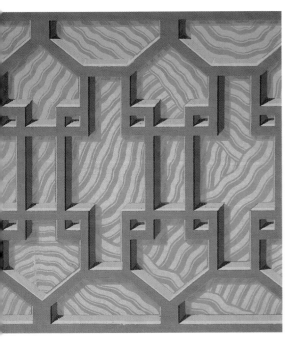

so in a different form. This time, rather than individual elements being gracefully blended into a Western framework, the emphasis was upon creating a complete environment, a Western idea of Eastern decoration.

Such a fabrication is Brighton Pavilion, rebuilt for the Prince of Wales first in Neoclassical taste, later, in 1801, in a tentative Chinese style and, finally, by John Nash from 1816, as the imaginative extravaganza it is today. Outwardly a blend of Islamic and Hindu architectural forms, with onion domes and minarets, its interiors have all the ingredients of this late flowering of Orientalism: bambooing, fretwork, lacquerwork, painted paper, woven silks, dragons and pagodas. Nothing classical remains, apart from the basic form of the rooms – and not even that in many cases.

The Far Eastern influence declined after Brighton. In its place there arose a fascination with Moorish design. Leighton House, London – built in the 1860s, with the Arab Hall added in the '80s – was a scholarly interpretation of a Moorish palace, with elaborate tiling and reasonably accurate architectural detailing. The exotic was now Near Eastern rather than Far Eastern and its realization was faithful and exact rather than imaginative.

ABOVE *This detail is taken from a wallpaper that was designed to be used above the baseboard in the Royal Pavilion at Brighton, England, and would have formed a continuous and enclosing band. Fretwork patterns like this – a hallmark of the 'Chinese Chippendale' style – recur throughout chinoiserie design. The background, in two strong yellows, is an authentically Chinese detail (to be seen in embroideries) transformed to the realms of fantasy by the overlay of a vaguely pagoda-shaped 'fence'.*

RIGHT *A nineteenth-century Moorish fantasy in the Palace of Het Loo in Holland displays the use of loosely interpreted Moorish details applied to European furniture shapes. Flat patterns, probably stencilled, are used on the joinery – the dado overdoor and door. These types of patterns were available in books such as Owen Jones'* Grammar of Ornament *(1856).*

Another wave of Orientalism in the 1870s and '80s was japonaiserie. The discovery of Japanese prints made fashionable a range of objects from Japan, from porcelain to fans, screens to silks. Enormous quantities of such objects – sometimes designed to European taste – were exported to Europe, but there was little Western copying, since authenticity was at least part of their appeal. To collect Japanese art and objects supposedly demonstrated aesthetic sensitivity and the influence of japonaiserie was widespread and pervasive. The 1880s also saw the production of quantities of bamboo furniture, cheap and often ingenious in design. Everything from hat-racks to *jardinières*, from beds and chairs to wardrobes and dressing tables, came in bamboo in a blending of the East with the Empire, a mass-market Orientalism.

The twentieth century has also seen its flirtations with the East. Chinese motifs and decoration, for example, were particularly popular in the 1930s when lacquered cocktail cabinets, lit by lamps covered in crepe de Chine, would stand on Chinese rugs in thousands of shop windows. More recently, kelims with bold folk designs, large floor cushions covered in richly textured Eastern fabrics and intricately patterned Indian bedspreads have held a particular fascination.

ABOVE *Panels of antique tiles in bright colours and with the sinuous patterns typical of Turkish ceramics, contribute to Lord Leighton's 1880s recreation of a Moorish Palace at Leighton House, London. Tulips, carnations, irises and hyacinths – all native flowers of the Eastern Mediterranean – add to the opulence of the designs.*

LEFT *The Moorish elements in this Spanish room, designed in 1925, are a reminder that Spain was part of Islam until 1492. Painted in distemper colours on plaster, a florid kind of Gothic style with definite Moorish leanings is enriched with exotic birds. The intense blue is balanced by the orange trompe l'oeil tracery.*

The Elements of the Oriental Room

The Oriental Room is not intended as an authentic simulation of an interior, whether Chinese or Japanese, of a particular period or style – rather it is an invention, a fantasy, which uses oriental motifs to suggest a different, more exotic world. The oriental themes that have recurred in decoration since the seventeenth century can now, of course, be reinterpreted and reintroduced in many different ways.

Three decorative approaches to the Oriental Room are explored below and are described as Chinoiserie, the Exotic and the Ethnic. Although many of the elements examined are common to all three, the attributes and overall effect of each are different. A Chinoiserie Room may well contain real oriental objects but will always, before any other consideration, be light and elegant. An Exotic Room, on the other hand, will be marked by a concentrated richness and will almost certainly use genuine material of some kind. As an exercise in eclecticism, an Ethnic Room can lack charm – but with a light touch and a little humour its elements can be used to create a room to enjoy.

CHINOISERIE

The Chinoiserie Room, light in colour, delicately patterned with flowers, birds and trees and inspired by the hand-painted papers of the eighteenth century, is suitable for less formal rooms – bedrooms, small sitting rooms and conservatories. This type of treatment is also effective where there is a strong connection with the outdoors.

Silk-covered walls have a subtle oriental association appropriate to the Chinoiserie Room. Paper-backed silk wallpapers are available but expensive. Simulating silk in paint is not difficult and the result almost looks better than the real thing. An added advantage is that there are no seams, unlike paper-backed silk where the joints are prominent.

The basic method is first to drag the wall vertically, and then, when this coat has dried, to drag the same colour horizontally. This is particularly effective when a pale colour is dragged over a dark one. The dragging itself should be fairly open to suggest the weave of the fabric, open enough so that the backgound colour remains apparent, even after two coats of dragging. (For more detailed information on cross-dragging, see page 38.)

Chinoiserie colours include celadon green, a porcelain colour (with a paler coat dragged over the top), straw yellow, similar to the colour of matting, and clear bright 'Sung' yellow, another porcelain colour. A painted finish using these colours can be made to look even more like silk by trimming the walls with a real upholstery border in woven braid or gimp.

Another successful means of recreating the mood and atmosphere of a Chinoiserie Room is by simulating Chinese wallpaper. Look for patterns which in colour, rhythm and scale have something of the right Eastern quality about them. A skilled artist can, of course, paint Chinese patterns freehand on the wall, or onto pieces of furniture. But a more realistic option is to stencil oriental motifs – birds, dragons, pagodas – in panels set within areas of plain wallpaper. Perhaps the most effective way of

Sage-green panelling, which might otherwise be unremarkable, makes a striking background for a host of oriental elements. The printed cotton used on the walls and as a valance has all the character of a hand-painted eighteenth-century paper of European manufacture. The stove's tiles have pagodas, the frieze panels could have a common source with details in the mirror frame (page 129), there is a Chinese rug and some oriental ceramics – and yet the room is totally European.

simulating chinoiserie patterns is to cover the walls with fabrics, such as Indian cotton bedspreads, which have the appropriate colouring and design. Indian bedspreads – mass-produced and therefore inexpensive – are often patterned with a 'Tree of Life' motif similar to that found on Chinese papers. Small sprigged patterns are also effective. (For how to batten fabric to a wall, see pages 78–81.) Panels of Chinese wallpaper are still made in Hong Kong, but are expensive and do not look like eighteenth-century wallpaper. There are also papers in production today that reproduce the European-printed eighteenth-century designs that were, in turn, based on Chinese originals.

Bamboo is an important feature of the fantasy oriental look. It occurs as a wall finish in many chinoiserie rooms, notably at Brighton Pavilion where there is even a cast-iron staircase balustrade that simulates bamboo. Until the mid-nineteenth century, bamboo was often simulated and the finish painted onto turned wood; later, real bamboo furniture was occasionally painted to make it look fake. There are endless variations of technique for bambooing, ranging from the decorative interpretations typical of Regency furniture to more realistic approaches. One easy method of creating bamboo borders is to paint paper strips in a pale buff colour and then use a No. 3 sable brush to draw on bamboo outlines and details in dark brown. A mid brown can be used to add shading.

Simulating bamboo

All four examples shown here are painted in gouache and varnished on lengths of half-round hardwood moulding, rubbed down and primed. Always allow one coat to dry before applying the next. Use two or three tones of a colour to mark the characteristic joints. It is the detail of leaf nodes or spots that differentiates the styles. From left to right:

Mottled bamboo The mottled pattern – much used for furniture in the nineteenth century – was produced when heat was applied to real bamboo.
1 Apply an undercoat in an opaque bright yellow ochre paint.
2 Glaze with a mixture of raw and burnt umber. Immediately remove a random pattern of 'dapples' with dry fingertips.
3 Repeat the process using the same mixture – the dapples should overlap in a haphazard manner.
4 Again using the same mixture, paint the rings – the darker colour of the rings is produced from the build-up of glaze.
5 Varnish.

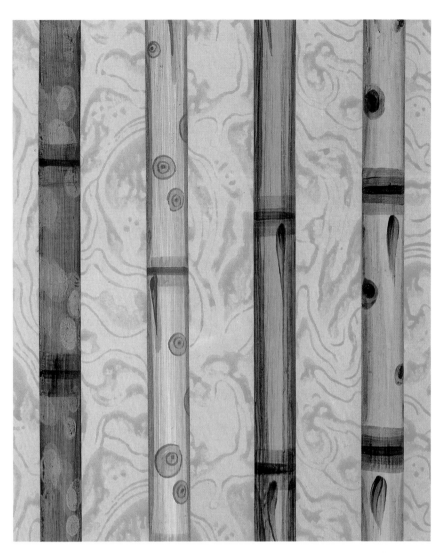

Red and White Early in the nineteenth century, large quantities of Chinese bamboo furniture were exported worldwide. The bamboo was given a thin white glaze and then picked out in vermilion.
1 Apply an undercoat in a dull stony buff paint.
2 Glaze with white.
3 Make a vermilion glaze and apply the wider rings and spots.
4 Using vermilion paint, apply the rings and leaf nodes and outline the spots.

5 Glaze completely with thin raw umber, wiped off the top so as to leave the sides shaded.
6 Varnish.

Natural This type of bamboo was often used for turned, painted beechwood furniture.
1 Apply the same undercoat as for mottled bamboo.
2 Using a glaze made from raw and burnt umber, paint in the wide rings and leaf nodes.
3 Using the same glaze, add the dark fine rings and shadows to the leaf nodes.
4 Glaze completely with thin raw umber, wiped off the top.
5 Varnish.

Green and White This effect is based on the furniture made for David Garrick by Chippendale (see page 129).
1 Apply an undercoat in white.
2 Using a weak bluish green glaze, paint in the wide rings, spots and leaf nodes.
3 In a darker glaze, paint narrower rings, the centres of the spots and the shadows of the leaf nodes.
4 Use an even darker glaze to paint in the fine details.
5 Glaze completely with thin raw umber, wiped off the top so as to leave the sides shaded.
6 Varnish.

EXOTIC RICHNESS

A different approach to that of the Chinoiserie Room is to create a rich, exotic and glittering jewel-box effect. Using lacquered finishes and gilding, the sumptuous appearance of Chinese screens can be recreated to produce a magical, enclosed environment appropriate for a study, a collector's room or a dining room. In the seventeenth and early eighteenth centuries, lacquer screens brought into Europe from the East were often dismantled and used as wall panelling, typically in rooms where collections of porcelain were displayed on wall brackets.

Lacquer – true oriental lacquer – was made from the sap of the tree *Rhus vernicifera*. It was applied in many thin, translucent coloured coats, polished, sometimes carved or inlaid with mother-of-pearl and often embellished with gold designs. In the West, from the seventeenth century, it was simulated in materials that came easily to hand – varnish, a similar substance, was most often used as the medium and the finish.

A rich, sumptuous finish, lacquer is used on furniture and screens and is usually executed in red or black. It can be adopted as a wall treatment to suggest rooms panelled in lacquerwork or as a suitably glowing background against which to display a collection of porcelain.

Several coats of blue glaze have been brushed over a smooth blue undercoat on the walls of this Exotic Room. Each of the glaze coats was slightly different from the others – some greener, some greyer. Finally, three coats of gloss varnish, untinted, were used to give a smooth and lustrous finish. The varnish has yellowed somewhat with time to give a distinctly jade green colour. The walls are edged with a wide woven-wool border. The sparkle of cut glass and the shine of the black lampshades complete the glittering ensemble. Gilding – shown here on the table and mirror – is a natural and effective accompaniment to lacquered finishes.

Lacquering walls

For lacquering to be successful, it is crucial that the background is well-prepared and completely smooth. Then, using successive glazes of translucent colour, the finish is built up until the colour is deep and even but still translucent; four coats or more may be required, brushed on freely and working vertically, diagonally and horizontally to cover the surface well. Each coat should be allowed to dry completely. After the final coat has dried, it is finished off with several coats of gloss varnish, rubbed down carefully between coats to build up to a lustrous finish. The example shown above has been painted in six stages over a white eggshell base. From left to right:

1 Make up a large quantity of glaze tinted strongly with cadmium orange and a little flat white to give it body. Brush this on loosely and evenly over the entire surface.

2 Add cadmium red artists' oil paint, diluted with turpentine, to the glaze and repeat the brushing.

3 Add crimson to the glaze and apply one coat. Allow to dry.

4 To make the colour darker, apply a second coat of glaze.

5 Mix a new glaze using Venetian red and apply one coat to achieve an even darker colour.

6 Make up a final, very weak glaze using black paint and apply to add strength and definition.

Several coats of gloss varnish will be needed to complete the process.

RIGHT *More than five coats of oil glaze were used to create this 'lacquered' dining room in a dark basement. The colour and finish are deliberately similar to the Chinese ceramic glaze called* sang de boeuf. *The owner wanted the walls to resemble aubergine-coloured leather. The undercoat was a strong, 'shocking' geranium red; I painted successive coats in a blackish purple glaze, some bluer, some quite black, to give depth to the colour. Three coats of clear gloss varnish reflect the light, and the colour of the off-white woodwork (which was dragged) is deliberately yellowish to link it to the sea-grass flooring.*

ETHNIC INFLUENCES

The third type of Oriental Room is Near and Middle Eastern rather than Far Eastern in inspiration and relies heavily on the use of fabric hangings. This version of Orientalism can be recreated using kelims with designs in attractive vegetable dyes, pennanted hangings and appropriately patterned fabrics layered on the wall in a manner which suggests the bazaar or the nomad's tent.

The flavour of the Middle East – of Islam – is also encapsulated in the rich, interlaced patterns of lattice and mosaic. The latticework screens seen in Moslem architecture, which break the fierce North African sunlight into intricately dappled patterns, give an atmosphere as evocative as that of Moorish tiles. The tiled mosaics of Morocco, where small geometrical pieces of tile, based on hexagons and octagons interlaced with pearly white strap-work, are built up into panels for dados, floors, or even whole walls. The special quality of these mosaics derives from the fact that the individual pieces are cut from larger tiles and never lie quite flat, thus allowing the light to flicker over the surface. Original Moorish tiling is handmade and, most characteristically, is turquoise, blue and white in colour.

RIGHT *Using Indian cotton bedspreads, blockprinted with a 'Tree of Life' pattern and hand-coloured, I transformed this featureless room into something Eastern and exotic. The bedspreads are stretched and fixed to battens on the walls. The valance and the trimming on the window blind are also Indian. Lacquered furniture and the straw mat and blind add to the catalogue of oriental influences. The white cotton curtains are reefed in imitation of curtains shown in an eighteenth-century watercolour of an English family's drawing room in India.*

LEFT *A bedspread, cut to frame a Moorish arch, introduces a hint of the Middle East in colour, pattern and, especially, shape, while the textures of whitewash and textiles, polished flags and pebble mosaic are nicely balanced.*

LEFT *Blue and white tiles, painted in a Spanish-Moorish pattern, encase the plumbing arrangements in this small bathroom. The uneven nature of the painting on the tiles, the simple Moorish fret of the cabinet door and the whitewashed walls, allied to the glitter of the tiled surfaces, capture the naive charm and practicality often sought in 'ethnic' schemes.*

LEFT *Tiles and tile-like patterns in a limited palette and executed in stencilling give a subtly Middle Eastern flavour to this bathroom designed by Renzo Mongiardino. Weight is given to the scheme by using more and more white as the bands of decoration rise to the ceiling. The shapes of the stencil echo those in the cut and polished mirrorglass frame.*

RIGHT *The characteristic shapes of Islamic architecture and the sparkling effect of tile mosaic shown here are immediately recognizable as Moorish. The contrasting colours of the distempered walls and the intricacies of the carved and painted woodwork – all examples of native crafts – evoke the atmosphere of Morocco.*

THE FITTED ROOM

Like a writing bureau with its array of drawers and pigeonholes, a Chinese cabinet with secret compartments and mirrored niches, or the eighteenth-century doctor's travelling medicine chest with slots for bottles and clips for instruments, the ideal Fitted Room embodies the kind of ingenuity and compression that has its own beauty and fascination. Combining neatness and intricacy, it encompasses both the wide-angled vision of the broad design and the fine focus of the exact fit.

Whether for books, clothes, or kitchen equipment, the Fitted Room fulfils storage and organizational needs in a considered, architectural way, which has its own decorative qualities. It is fitted out in appropriate materials of fine quality, carefully chosen and beautifully finished, and attention to detail is evident not only in the way the room 'works' but also in its every component – every hinge, dovetail and knob, every drawer and door. To accomplish this requires a high standard of craftsmanship allied to sensitive, imaginative design and planning that takes into account the specific demands of the job in hand.

Many traditional storage solutions arose to meet specific needs. This is why they are so appealing – and why we may look to them for inspiration when designing fitted rooms today. Almost every Victorian shop, for example, had its own system of organization, specifically tailored to its merchandise. Banks of small drawers in apothecaries' stores housed powders and packets, while potions were ranged in beautifully labelled matching jars on special shelves; chests and airtight containers held spices and dry goods in grocers' stores; carefully subdivided shelves, trays and drawers in haberdashers' shops stored buttons, needles and reels of thread. The intricate, space-saving details from the interiors of old boats, trains and caravans, even nineteenth-century mechanical furniture – chairs that unfold to become library steps or beds that swing out from the wall – may inspire solutions for neatly detailed and finished fitted storage in modern homes where space is often at a premium.

By stark contrast, many modern commercial ranges of system shelving or 'fitted' kitchen units fail to accommodate the specific characteristics of the items they are required to house. Worse, since they are imposed, imported and often intrusive solutions, they tend to

A synthesis of ingenuity and compactness, the successful Fitted Room is one in which function and appearance are skilfully combined. I designed these floor-to-ceiling bookshelves to be both practical and aesthetically pleasing. They are supported by the narrowest struts possible and dressed at the top with a polystyrene cornice and at the bottom with a minimal baseboard, barely more than a kicking strip. Articulation comes from the varied widths and the breaks in the plan of the shelving. Two shelves are used as a cabinet – disguised by fake spines which are stuck to black-papered doors. The space above the double doorway is used for large books laid flat.

Facciata del cecondo muro della ftanza

The ultimate in one-room living, this design by the Dutch engineer/inventor Cornelius Meyer is a late-seventeenth-century solution to the problem of fitting into a confined space all the obsessions of the owner at the same time as producing a functional room. With the closets' doors shut, this would have been a plain panelled room – yet they open to reveal a treasury of ingenious practical inventions including a bed concealed in an alcove (22), cabinets for tools, clothes, crockery and linen (27–30), guns and knives (32), a thermometer (33), dirty and fresh linen (34–5) and a secret stairway (36).

obscure, or even destroy, the architectural integrity of the room. Moreover, to make them appear attractive and eyecatching in advertisements they often have over-elaborate details where restraint would be more effective. This is what makes many so-called fitted kitchens unsuccessful as rooms.

Shelving, which represents the most basic form of fitting out, is best approached in one of two ways. Either it may be reduced in emphasis so that it reads as part of the room's basic structure, and so becomes an integral part of the room, or it can be wholeheartedly expressed and treated as an introduction, almost as a piece of furniture. Shelving which is neither properly built in and integrated nor fully expressed will always look awkward and hesitant.

If it is to be treated as part of the room, shelving is often best set into recesses, such as the alcoves on either side of a chimney breast. Within these confines it is easier to make a wall of shelves that is an integral part of the room, in harmony with its style, scale and rhythm.

The alternative approach is to design and colour shelves or closets so that they stand out from their surroundings. If this is done, the original room still remains to be read complete in itself. The failure to distinguish between these two approaches is the most common cause of the failure in fitting-out.

Closets are often built in with shelving so that concealed storage is combined with open display. They, too, can be thought of as furniture, constructed and detailed as such, or, alternatively, built in so that they become the walls – the confines of the room – and decorated accordingly. In either case, closets usually work best within a scheme of shelving if they extend either up to dado height (about 75–90cm/ 30–36in) or to full room height – topped off with a cornice, or whatever is appropriate in the context of the rest of the room. These two horizontal divisions have, by tradition and long association, become accepted as natural.

This wall of pale wood strips (BELOW LEFT) *is in fact a set of drawers specially designed to hold a collection of stamps* (BELOW RIGHT) *– out of the light and dust, but accessible. The cabinet looks like a louvred wall and forms an effective room divider.*

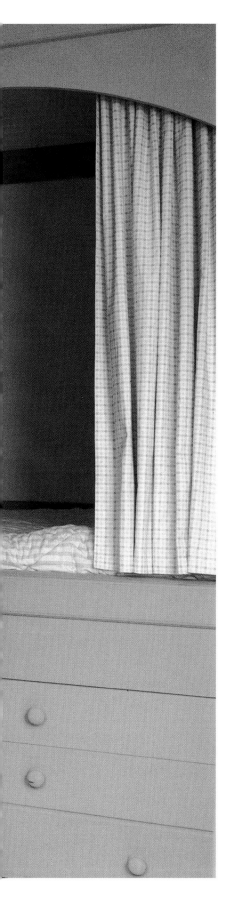

LEFT *This modern box bed, whose drawers not only hold spare bedding but also pull out to act as steps, draws inspiration from European folk precedent – beds were often built into walls in modest houses. The simple colour scheme, the turned wooden knobs and the boarded ceiling are all features that could easily be adapted to suit different types of room.*

ABOVE *In building out the chimney breast in this playroom I used the otherwise wasted space above the mantelpiece for a small cabinet. By hingeing it at the top, the door can carry a picture quite safely. The mantelpiece is an old one, re-used. The cornice is of expanded polystyrene and the angle beads are of wood – the use of wood beads was a commonplace in the nineteenth century and they have a strong visual impact.*

LEFT *A narrow and essentially featureless passage has been converted into a useful storage area through the introduction of a wall of panelled closets. A traditional chequered floorcloth adds visual interest.*

RIGHT *The architectural impact and composition of these closets is the most significant feature of this sitting room. The closets, by being built forward from the chimney breast, have caused the fireplace to be tucked into an intimate alcove. The large closets have their own rhythm and character and could be fitted out inside with anything from a shower or kitchenette to the smallest of collections.*

LEFT *The walls of the seventeenth-century library at Langley Marish in Buckinghamshire, England, are entirely cupboarded. The room is a model of ingenuity and finish. Sir John Kederminster built the 'secret' library and fitted the walls with shelved cupboards whose doors were painted with elaborate cartouches, portraits and trompe l'oeil books. Successful both as a library and as a room, it is full of the richness and singlemindedness that make the seventeenth century such a marvellous hunting ground for design ideas.*

LIBRARIES AND BOOKSHELVES

A fascinating testament to the way in which room fittings have evolved to meet new and changing needs is supplied by the library, one of the best examples of the Fitted Room. In medieval times, books, treasured and rare, were propped against lecterns or laid flat on shelves. In cathedral libraries – the 'public' libraries of the day – they were often chained to the desks. A small collection of books might be kept in a chest or cupboard, known as a 'press'. By the late seventeenth century the ownership of books was no longer uncommon. The sheer quantity of books being printed meant that any literate person's library could fill more than a shelf or drawer. The diarist Samuel Pepys organized his books by size and kept them standing on shelves in bookcases with doors glazed like windows. Designed as pieces of furniture, freestanding and movable, such bookcases to some extent set the pattern for subsequent fitted shelving. The library as a shelved, as opposed to a cupboarded, room emerged during the eighteenth century. The craftsmanship and design skills of the time were employed to create architecturally inspired bookcases and shelving which reflected the classical arrangement of wall space. In the nineteenth century, the library became more of a family room, furnished with writing tables and deep leather armchairs and a combination of glazed and open shelving.

Shelves should be scaled to suit the size of the books or objects which are being stored or displayed, so that they appear neither cramped nor lost. It is usual to graduate the size of shelves, with the tallest shelves for the largest objects nearest to the floor. Books, especially, are very heavy, and the design must allow enough support for shelves which are thick enough not to sag. Conservationists would call for a gap behind the books for air to circulate, and aesthetes would demand shelves deep enough for the spines to be fully on the shelves. In general, constraints imposed on the design will result in a vertical emphasis – which is often the happiest kind for a richly conceived and executed interior.

To finish off the shelves, and to keep dust away from books or the

RIGHT *Generous shelves, boldly designed and finished with just enough shine for the chosen colour, form a whole wall incorporating doors and radiators. The grilles, simple and original, are reminiscent of eighteenth-century food cupboards and the small sliding shelf which supports a bronze helmet is precisely the kind of useful detail that is essential for a working fitted room.*

objects displayed on them, one can adopt the traditional dust frill or fringe – a scalloped leather edging fixed to the front edge or underside of the shelf to prevent dust from settling on the tops of the books below. A dust frill makes shelving look neater and it also gives some horizontal emphasis to balance the strong verticals.

An amusing treatment for cabinets built in amongst shelves is to give them the appearance of open bookshelves by painting their fronts with trompe l'oeil books or even sticking real book spines in position. This is an effective way of breaking up a large expanse of wooden doors. Alternatively, half-round wooden moulding strips painted in different colours or covered with strips of leather, cloth or decorative paper, can be lettered with fake titles and applied to a dark background. Varying the heights of the 'books', with some leaning at slight angles, makes for greater realism. Perhaps the most enjoyable part of this game is inventing the titles. There are many examples of eighteenth- and nineteenth-century libraries where jib-doors have been treated as trompe bookshelves, with tooled leather spines displaying authors' names and wonderfully whimsical titles (*Simple Deceit* by A. Carpenter, for instance). In a modern library, a mix of real or fake dust jackets and coloured cloths would be more credible than leather spines.

RIGHT *A neatly detailed closet like this, incorporating shelves, a radiator behind a woven brass grille, and a closet behind a door painted with fake leather books, calls for some equally detailed paintwork. Fine veneers with ebony or boxwood lines or tortoiseshell (as here) are appropriate to the elegant edging with its well-thought-out corners.*

LEFT *A closet front – painted to look like books and with a real leather bookmark acting as a handle – opens out to form a bedside table. It is supported by a quarter-round stay. This little* jeu d'esprit *(and its pair on the other side of the bed) is decorated to match the old leather books that surround them.*

Simulating tortoiseshell

There are many different ways of painting tortoiseshell. This technique uses the traditional method of gouache diluted in beer and the final effect is of soft, toffee-coloured diagonal banding. Red or green could also be used as background colours. This sample is in three stages.

1 Paint the background (left) in a yellow flat oil paint. Make up a very thin glaze using burnt umber mixed with beer. Brush the glaze over the surface to wet it thoroughly but do not use so much that it runs.

2 Make up a second, thicker, glaze using burnt umber thinned only slightly with beer. While the first glaze is still wet, quickly dash in 'continents', 'islands' and 'archipelagoes' of this second glaze and immediately soften with a badger brush (middle).

3 While this is still wet add some very dark, barely diluted, blobs of burnt umber to the centre of each 'landmass'. Soften again (right).

4 Complete when dry with two or three coats of varnish. Rub down each coat lightly.

KITCHENS

A dresser and an armoire in the corner set the scene for this French kitchen and dominate the working arrangements on the right which, by their plain and functional lines, retire into insignificance. The armoire has the capacity to hold vast quantities of goods and could even be ventilated through the outside wall to provide a food cupboard.

One of the most satisfying pieces of storage furniture is undoubtedly the traditional kitchen dresser, satisfying perhaps because implicit in its basic structural division of closed cupboard with open shelves above are the comfortable and familiar proportions of dado, wall area and cornice. In many old kitchens, dressers were not self-contained, movable pieces of furniture but were built in, so it is not surprising that they should echo the architectural divisions of the room. When they were painted in with the wall, the connection was further emphasized.

A dresser works well because its design caters for several specific functions. The cupboard at the base accommodates large pieces of

Nineteenth-century order is here expressed in neat and elegant lettering and high-quality metalwork. There is a place for everything and the housekeeper's strict eye would no doubt see to it that everything was in its place. The large metal canisters run on casters. The tall, narrow cupboards are for hanging sugar-loaves.

equipment or crockery; drawers, sometimes subdivided and lined in baize, take cutlery and folded linen; the top provides a worksurface for preparing food and shelves for jugs, plates and bowls, with rails for displaying plates and hooks for cups. The sheer efficiency of the piece and the visual appeal of the open shelves crammed with patterned china could not be further from the majority of modern fitted kitchen units, standardized to manufacturers' specifications but not, in the end, scaled to any practical function and woefully lacking in charm.

Dressers, whether original or reproduction, are expensive, and old ones are sometimes so tall and bulky that they have to be cut down to fit into modern kitchens. A practical, and cheaper, alternative is to do as was often done in the past and simply attach a plate rack or shelving to the wall above a cupboard, painting both parts to match. This is, after all, the essence of the dresser.

Other fittings tailored to the specific activities that take place in the kitchen include metal racks, like the overhead rails used in old butchers' shops for hanging utensils, pots and pans; wall-mounted plate-draining racks; butcher's block chopping tables with their capacious bottom shelves. All these serve their individual purposes well and help to make a kitchen a more personal and efficient place in which to work and live.

Few homes today have the space for the type of room specialization that was a feature of High Victorian country houses, whose 'below stairs' offices could run to a dozen different rooms, each fitted out for a specific function: still room, larders for game, fish and preserves, butler's pantry, housekeeper's room, laundry, boot room, even a room where newspapers were ironed before being put on the library table, and so on, all in addition to the main kitchen. Yet despite the pressure on space, many people today are returning to the notion of keeping a separate cool larder for storing food in a more natural form of

refrigeration. Ideally, such a larder should have three external walls so that it is surrounded by cooling air, and slate or marble shelves and a stone floor to help maintain low temperatures. It can be fitted with hooks on which to hang cured meats, and so on. Fulfilling no other function, the larder can be fitted out specifically to meet particular food storage needs.

A utility room, perhaps adapted from an old scullery, can be similarly fitted out to house noisy and visually disruptive modern machinery – such as washing machines and tumble driers – thus freeing space in the main kitchen. And since we all seem to live our lives in our kitchens these days there is all the more reason to make it a room that is livable in. If the presence of all that machinery is unavoidable in the kitchen it could perhaps be grouped together, rather than spread out, so that other, more attractive, things are those that occupy our attention when we are using the room or sitting at the table.

ABOVE *A well-organized storage system is a visual catalogue. The more precise the needs, the more precise will be the result. Here goods and kitchenware have transformed an entire wall, neatly wrapping round a window. Everything is simple, functional and strong.*

LEFT *I lined this small chimney alcove with French tiles and fitted it with a closet. The area is used as a buffet and houses all manner of things for the table. The two cutlery drawers were fashioned from knife trays and there is room for fruit, cheese, jam and so on. The closet is kept discreet and faceless by having its mouldings reduced to the minimum.*

FAR LEFT *Tongued and grooved boarding makes a whole wall of closets and two freestanding 'units'. Visual emphasis on the wall, free of knobs and handles, is played down. The area between the two islands and the refrigerator – which is tucked into the wooden wall and invisible from the table – is used for cooking and preparation.*

BATHROOMS

The bathroom is a relatively modern room, with little in the way of decorative traditions. The first of two broad approaches is to opt for a modern aesthetic, with hard surfaces and precision finishes, possibly looking to the 1930s for inspiration; the second is to furnish and decorate the bathroom as any other room, allowing its functional side to remain incidental to the overall effect. When bathrooms were first incorporated into nineteenth-century houses, they were decorated in much the same fashion as bedrooms and, since they were frequently found on the same floor, this approach had a certain logic to it. In many bathrooms the airing cupboard built round the hot-water tank forms an intrusive block – usually in a corner. If there is enough room the whole wall can be built out, swallowing the tank and the pipes and providing a wall of warm, dry storage. Towel rails can be installed, nearest the tank. Such a range of cabinets is often the most economical way of providing storage, and the lost floor space is amply compensated by the advantages. A skilled and imaginative carpenter could, with ingenuity, give the whole room a distinctive character.

Who uses the room will dictate to a large extent the storage requirements: a family with young children might need to provide space

The versatility of matchboarding is as well illustrated here as the need for careful organization of functions. In this compact bathroom and dressing room, the wall has been pulled forward, leaving a basin alcove and lavatory recess and room for a closet. The cistern, pipes and clothes are concealed above, below and between. The room is finished in a dry-looking white paint.

for bathtime playthings as well as towels, cleaning materials, cosmetics, dirty linen, and so on – much of which needs to be protected from dust or condensation. A bathroom that is entirely lined with built-in closets and fittings, each carefully tailored to one of these many specific needs, demands a high level of craftsmanship if a seamless, integrated finish is to be achieved.

Even if the emphasis is less functional and rather on creating the impression of a furnished room, some fitting out will usually be necessary to provide adequate storage space. This may often, at the same time, conceal plumbing arrangements. If the same facing material is used throughout, it provides a degree of visual unity. Tongued and grooved panelling, for example, could be taken across the front of the bath and wash basin and behind the lavatory as well as being used as a front for closets. The panelling could be painted to blend with the walls or treated as a decorative element on its own. Thus even an informal approach can fulfil the requirements of a successful Fitted Room.

Traditional items of storage furniture can be introduced into bathrooms that are truly room-sized: armoires for linen and towels, blanket chests and large wicker baskets are all versatile and appealing, and if organized with care will fulfil the role of fitments.

Any built-in furniture in a half-timbered room would prove intrusive, so here it seemed best to build out. I drew inspiration for the design of these two tall closets from the idea of a medieval gatehouse. The hot-water tank is housed in the left-hand tower, clothes in the right. The doors are of broomstick dowels backed with stretched cotton to allow ventilation. Another closet, a wardrobe, in the same house was designed as a medieval tent, complete with a pointed 'roof'.

DRESSING ROOMS

Clothes storage, like kitchen storage, does not present a single, uniform requirement: hats, shoes, dresses, suits, shirts, jackets and ties need to be stored in different ways and take up different amounts of space. Most efficient and space-saving in the long run is to borrow floor area from a bedroom and create a walk-in closet. Another possibility is to fit out a small spare room or box room to take account of all the various requirements. A combination of hanging rails, drawers, shelves and racks can be constructed, with details copied from shop fittings; the room will also need a mirror and a set of steps for reaching the top shelves. Such fitted 'rooms', like the housekeeper's room in the Victorian country house, or old linen rooms lined with cedar wood, are exceptionally pleasant places in their own right, with their neat detailing and air of practicality.

Most people, however, do not have the option of converting a whole room for clothes storage, and rely on a combination of wardrobes and chests of drawers. In the eighteenth century, the forerunner of the wardrobe, the clothes press, in which clothes were stored flat, was used in conjunction with simple round pegs fixed to the wall. Shaker peg-boards, fixed around the room at picture-moulding height, reflect this

ABOVE *The eighteenth-century approach to detail is exemplified by these humble brass cloakpins. Intended originally for hanging clothes they were also used by the upholsterer in pairs beside windows, first, both together on one side to tie the ropes of pull-up curtains and, later, one on each side, for holding tie-backs. The shell cloakpin (second from the top) dates from the 1750s, those of Neoclassical design (top and bottom) are somewhat later and the turned pair is probably from around 1760.*

RIGHT *Crisp detailing on the stairs of a nineteenth-century row house. The traditional spot for a built-in closet — on the landing, at the top of the stairs — is possibly the only way that clothes storage can be neatly and successfully managed in some houses.*

LEFT *A clothes closet displays its logic at a glance. The execution of the design should be as faultless as the concept. Clothes and shoes are nearest to hand, while a ladder is required to reach objects such as suitcases and top hats.*

tradition. The pegs, known as cloakpins, were either whittled by hand or turned. In more affluent homes, they were of turned or cast brass, sometimes with elaborate and decorative heads. These elegant and often beautifully finished cloakpins were also used as cleats for tying off the cords of festoon curtains.

In the nineteenth century, clothes were generally kept in wardrobes and by the beginning of the twentieth century, these had developed into ingenious and intricately detailed affairs, with sliding shelves for folded clothes, tie racks, boxes for collar studs, rails for hanging clothes, hooks and drawers, often neatly labelled. The interiors of steamer trunks, lined in cotton ticking or plaid, display the same meticulous attention to detail. A similar quality can be found today in some shop fittings, where each different item of clothing has been carefully allocated its own specific storage system.

CONCEALMENT

It is not dishonest to want to hide the elements of servicing of the house in order to maintain the integrity of the room. It is important, however, that the strategies adopted for concealing the plumbing, electrical and heating works, and their attendant wires, pipes, tubes, ducts and outlets, whatever form they take, grow out of the detail and proportion of the room. Piecemeal additions always draw attention to themselves and so defeat the point of the exercise.

The principle can be illustrated by the common practice of boxing in pipework. For this to work well, the result must look considered, part of the architectural detailing of the room. If the boxing stops where the pipe stops, it will be all too obvious and awkward in appearance. If, on the other hand, the boxing is continued to make a low ledge or shelf, or brought up to waist height to make a dado panel, it will merge with the room as a whole.

Particularly neat ways of concealing pipes and bell wires, while leaving them accessible, were devised in Victorian times. Ducts let into

ABOVE *Strategies for disguise can be as humorous as they are ingenious. Here, sliding shutters, which run on small wooden wheels inset into their bottom edges, disappear behind the bookcases – when they are closed they look like curtains, painted to match the real curtains on other windows in the same room. Cabinets and a radiator are within the dado area. The painted marble beam and columns were added to give visual support to the scheme. Cupboards such as these, with their slight cockbeads (small mouldings of semi-circular section), have been made much easier to construct since the invention of coreboard.*

RIGHT *A radiator cover, tied in with the decorative scheme at dado height, forms a useful display shelf. The same treatment could accommodate plumbing, or just a cabinet.*

the wall to accommodate pipework were covered with a board screwed in place, which could be removed from time to time for inspection. The edge of the board was finished with a bead and the surface painted in with the wall. The bead made the joint between wall and board look neater, by making it appear deliberate – a far better approach than simply leaving it unfinished. The same idea could be adapted for a ceiling hatch giving access to an attic. Instead of being framed with an architrave, the hatch can be dropped to align with the ceiling and trimmed with a bead.

A MACHINE FOR LIVING IN

Le Corbusier's famous statement that 'the house is a machine for living in', is usually interpreted as the modern architect championing soulless mechanized surroundings. In fact it is a recommendation of the notion of control: if the house is indeed a machine, then we should be able to direct its functions and appearance to suit our needs and preferences. The best fitted rooms do precisely this.

A ladder (ABOVE LEFT) *gives access to a sleeping platform above a playroom and allows an otherwise redundant space to be utilized. It folds away, flat to the wall* (ABOVE RIGHT). *The design of this ladder was inspired by one in Prague, but it would have delighted the engineer/inventor Cornelius Meyer (see page 148).*

THE COLLECTOR'S ROOM

The Collector's Room, like its near relative the Fitted Room, has as its starting point the organization of things. In the case of the Fitted Room, the need is for practical and accessible storage, an organizational system that makes a room work. In the Collector's Room, however, the intention is to display, to show off treasures, even to inspire wonder. Early conventions of display provide useful clues as to the best ways of arranging paintings and *objets d'art*. But whatever the interests of the modern collector in interior decoration and in the display of the collection, his or her attitude will give the Collector's Room its own unique character. The possibilities for collection and display are limitless – but somewhere lies a compromise whereby collection and interior are successfully fused to ensure that rooms which are full of interest and which express the passion of the collector are still convincing and enjoyable interiors.

THE CABINET OF CURIOSITIES

The roots of the Collector's Room go back to the *Wunderkammer* or 'cabinet of curiosities' of the sixteenth century, the collections of things exotic, curious or beautiful assembled by scholars and noblemen. Sometimes small enough to be arranged on a few shelves, such collections generally occupied a private cabinet or closet, and might include corals, shells, animal skulls, relics, miniature paintings, fossils, ancient coins and weapons, arranged in still-lifes. Although to us the contents of these treasure troves may seem diverse and disparate, there was a unifying intellectual basis to them: they were intended as a microcosm of the three kingdoms, animal, vegetable and mineral. The vogue for collecting evolved from the pursuit of knowledge. Painters' houses – and especially their studios – still exhibit a similar attitude. Skulls and bones, plants, postcards and cuttings, sculpture and *objets trouvés* can become at once the decoration, the work in progress and the diary. They form the entire environment.

Natural history specimens were amassed by early collectors, either through a desire to categorize and catalogue, or solely as a means by which to decorate and embellish. In the Rococo grottoes of the eighteenth century, shells, minerals and corals, no longer the curiosities

The collectors of works of art will be almost as concerned with the arrangement of their collection and its setting as with its intrinsic beauty. Such collectors create rooms that form a whole environment – a place for contemplation as well as conversation. In this sitting room, every available space is used for display and every object is part of the collection. The effect is rich and ordered and at the same time hardly 'decorated' at all. The collector's selective eye ensures the room's homogeneity.

they had been in the Renaissance, were used to create organic and often eccentric compositions.

Throughout the nineteenth century the hallways of English country houses were hung with animal skins and hunters' trophies, collections which were themselves a tribute to the era of Empire and exploration – symbols *par excellence* of conquest and control. Collecting was a popular, an obsessive pastime in the nineteenth century and embraced all spheres of life. The acquisitiveness of the age was expressed in the amateur naturalist's neatly labelled drawers of insects and fossils, in the bibliophile's complete editions marshalled on library shelves and in the sentimental devotion to ephemera which cluttered every middle-class Victorian dining room.

The South Kensington Museum, London, later renamed the Victoria & Albert Museum, was founded in the 1860s as a museum for the applied arts. The museum made the display of public collections enormously influential on the decoration of houses in the latter part of the nineteenth century. Its rooms were to be decorated by leading practitioners of the applied arts with the famous Green Room being

This collection of pictures and objects connected with falconry has a strong unity of theme and purpose, yet the effect is curiously heterogenous. It is the important-looking pieces of furniture, rather than the way in which the collection itself is displayed that, by their strength and decorative qualities, give the room its character.

commissioned from William Morris's company – Morris, Marshall, Faulkner & Co. – in 1866. Each room or gallery was itself to be regarded as part of the exhibit – collection and decoration were inseparable.

In our century, the line between collecting and decorating has become irretrievably blurred. The display of a collection, with its contribution of colour, pattern and form and the appeal of individual pieces massed for visual impact, is, after all, another way of creating a room. Today, magazines, books and films, rather than museums, provide inspiration and the way we use, or reject, the many examples available to us must be the result of our individual response. However, in any collection, whether of pictures or of objects, there should be a unifying scale, theme or even colour for the collection to look homogenous. A collection of objects based on an historical character, for instance, would be homogenous in theory but would have no visual unity. For any ensemble to be unified, the objects must be considered from the perspective of shared visual qualities.

A shoal of fish darting across rough plasterwork and 'threatened' by ancient fish-spears forms part of a collection of folk art. The arrangement is a humorous and personal reinterpretation of a natural history collection.

ABOVE *Ancient stone and terracotta objects and a wooden burial casket are crowded against walls and on shelves whose rough textures and stony colours harmonize perfectly with them. The burial masks are mounted so that they catch the light and cast soft shadows.*

RIGHT *This collection of early American folk art – pictures, samplers, carvings and everyday objects linked by their age and origins – is arranged neither as a museum nor to look like an early American home. Here the collection is the decoration and* vice versa. *The white-painted walls and matchboarding, the terracotta cupboard doors and plain tiled floor make their own understated contribution.*

Collecting and Displaying Pictures

There is a series of Dutch paintings dating from the first half of the seventeenth century showing rooms in which pictures are hung all over the walls, often with a table in the foreground holding more paintings and sculpture. The walls are densely hung, but otherwise the room is bare. This 'postage stamp' approach to hanging, while it lessens the impact of each picture, gives a unified effect to the walls and allows the overall collection to make its statement as a collection. Many of these pictures are records of particular rooms set up as galleries for the display of a collection. Others are more of an inventory, an imaginary depiction of all that a collector had accumulated – a 'snapshot' proof of ownership.

Nevertheless, at this time pictures were not consciously arranged but were simply amassed in large rooms. For example, in the early seventeenth century Lord Arundel's collection of pictures and sculpture was on show in a long upper gallery, the type of room typically used for exercise in inclement weather.

Many small pictures in the early seventeenth century were set off by highly finished frames, inlaid with tortoiseshell and ebony and intricately recessed, exhibiting all the hallmarks of inlaid furniture of the period. Such intricacy and elaboration related to the background against which pictures were displayed – Italian cut velvet; Spanish leather, embossed, painted and gilded; panelling – with the frame forming a border between picture and room. Small and intricate paintings, as these often were, need to be surrounded by other intricacies for the sake of an evenly balanced and textured room. Alternatively, changes in scale can prevent the paintings from being swamped by their surroundings. Later in the seventeenth century, norms for the display of paintings began to be established. There was a growing tendency to group pictures thematically: landscapes were hung with landscapes, portraits with other portraits. Standard canvas sizes came to be adopted.

One effect of Palladianism was to make the display of a painting part of the architectural organization of a room. A painting was the most important 'panel' of a panelled wall and its frame, richly gilded or painted, reflected this. The background against which a collection of pictures was displayed was often a strong red. With the Rococo, the frame became more closely linked to furniture styles and to the decorative plaster mouldings which swept over ceilings and walls; generally made of carved wood, gessoed and gilded in a highly ornate fashion, it became fully integrated with the decor. By the beginning of the nineteenth century, however, frames had ceased to be regarded as part of the room's detailing and were related solely to the picture.

This room in Moscow, stuffed with aristocratic memorabilia, is redolent of faded grandeur and old traditions. The arrangement of the pictures is subject to conventions which just save the room from being cluttered: the largest canvases, tilted forward to make them easier to see, are hung below the cornice; a second row of smaller pictures is just above chairback-height and the gaps between are sprinkled with tiny things. The blue of the walls is a match for the mass of pictures and objects.

Collections of prints were treated somewhat differently. Eighteenth-century print collections were framed with utmost simplicity, in uniform black wooden mouldings with little or no gilding. Prints were tightly framed, often showing no white border. Displaying deep white borders around prints came into fashion only towards the end of the nineteenth century with the popularity of signed editions of etchings: a print lost value if the border was cut off. The effect, however, was to make a display of prints look rather 'spotty' – quite different from the denser and more even effect of the earlier style of framing.

Gentlemen returning from the Grand Tour of Europe would often bring back with them a portfolio of engravings of Old Masters, views of Italy and antiquarian subjects. The print room evolved as a way of displaying these collections, and enjoyed a vogue during the latter part of the eighteenth century. The engravings were pasted directly onto the walls of a room, most often a small, informal 'closet' or bedroom, rather than a more important room. Set out in groups or columns and sharing a theme, the prints' basic arrangement would be enriched with a variety of other elements – paper borders, bows, knots, swags and garlands of flowers, all printed for just such a purpose. The borders and ornaments were monochrome, like the prints, while the background wall-colour was usually pale – 'straw', 'cane' or a light green or blue.

RIGHT *Tall, narrow panels are accentuated by a set of prints hung in columns. They retain their old gilt frames and their uneven, handmade glass, which creates reflections with a mysterious quality that gives an added layer of interest impossible to achieve with modern glass. A jib-door is disguised by the strength of the pattern of prints and panels.*

BELOW *When the print room was in vogue (c. 1760–1820) 'cane-colour' or 'straw-colour' was one of the usual background colours for the prints. This modern print room, with its dark dado, continues that tradition. The prints themselves, selected for their common subject matter and sympathetic tones, are linked by paper 'ropes' and ornaments.*

LEFT *A rigidly symmetrical arrangement of nineteenth-century pictures is hung on a wallpaper of a nineteenth-century design. The paper provides a kind of grid for the pictures and has been carefully hung to line up with the gilt frame of the looking glass. The Balinese masks, which fill up the centre of the composition, lose something of their extravagant foreignness by being tonally close to the wallpaper and are thereby absorbed into the group.*

To make a print room today, if it is impossible to assemble a collection of old engravings, it is better to use reproductions than to attempt to recreate the effect with modern prints. Alternatively, one can use photocopies treated with tea or a wash of raw umber to dull the paper and simulate the effect of age. Modern versions of borders, swags and so on are available from specialist suppliers and you can make them yourself by cutting out the decorative frames surrounding old engravings and photocopying them onto good quality laid paper. The prints should be stuck in place with starch paste so that they can be removed at a later date if required.

HANGING PICTURES

In early public museums, collections of paintings were no longer hung with the architectural characteristics of a room in mind or to suit individual taste, but academically, by period or school of painting, and in this century it has become the custom to display works of art in bland, featureless white or off-white rooms, settings which supposedly do not detract from what is on display. While such an environment may suit some modern works, there is a new approach in museum circles which

RIGHT *Red textiles are a traditional background for pictures. In this room I had to accommodate a large collection of pictures, which are linked by a shared style of framing and by their similar colouring. That the grouping is not strictly symmetrical does not matter – it is the shape of the arrangement that is important. The main group is centred on the wall with the pictures in its right-hand column set on the jib-door. I used red ropes to hang most of the pictures in this room for vertical emphasis and to help unify the groups. The picture rail has been placed right up against the ceiling.*

The chimney breast of any room is the focus (the latin word for 'hearth') of that room and will always attract the collector's most considered objects. Here, an eclectic assortment of pieces of quality is kept in balance by the interplay of dark and light, of statuary, relief and flat canvas, and above all by rich surfaces set against plain cream walls. No 'rules' can be adduced from this kind of arrangement except, perhaps, that there are no rules, and that it is often only by trying things out that harmony is achieved.

favours a return to strong, richly coloured backgrounds for paintings of an earlier date, more suggestive of those rooms in which the pictures would first have been seen. For the most part, it is to earlier conventions rather than to public displays that one must look for clues as to the best way to arrange pictures in a private space today.

Hanging pictures is a way of introducing rhythm and pattern to a room. A collection of pictures of similar size will unify a wall when equally spaced out along it, whereas an arrangement centred on one large picture will effectively divide the wall into three parts, with an important central focus. The more minor right and left parts can then, of course, have their own less important arrangements. To introduce the measured effect of pictures hung as panels, panelling can be suggested in painted lines or in lengths of braid applied to the walls at regular intervals. Pictures hung in this way measure out a room.

Large paintings need visual breathing space and adequate viewing distance which is why, in the traditional arrangement, a sequence of full-length portraits displayed down a long gallery benefited from the scale of the architecture. In less spacious quarters, a chimney breast or alcove can provide the necessary framework for display.

Frames, like pictures, are effective if they display some kind of stylistic affinity. Certain styles of frame have also become inextricably linked with certain styles of paintings and, to the modern eye, elaborate framing has come to signify the presence of that which is precious and valuable. When framing prints or drawings, it is customary to set off the picture with a mount, the colour of which should be chosen with great care so that it enhances the drawing or print. The practice of painting fine wash lines on mounts to bring the mount colour closer to the dominant colour of the drawing is a useful refinement.

Pictures have been hung in different ways at different times. The modern way, using concealed rings, wires or cords and hooks or nails, is undoubtedly neat, but can leave one wondering how the pictures stay up. The eighteenth century was often more logical – well-made brass rings screwed into the top of the frame were dropped over brass-headed nails driven into the wall. Cords or chains made the method of hanging quite clear and, moreover, had their own impact – adding a slight vertical emphasis. The nineteenth-century picture moulding, like the eighteenth-century rod, allowed pictures to be moved easily and likewise employed coloured cords or decorative chains.

In a pale, sculptural room a set of architectural prints, framed alike in thin dark mouldings and hung in formal patterns, provides the decoration on the walls, to which they are linked by their wide white borders. The scheme is strengthened by the bronzes, while colour, pattern and softness are concentrated in the furnishing.

Collecting and Displaying Objects

Another strand of collecting and display involves objects, from fine porcelain, statues and antiquarian relics to the Victorian amateur naturalist's birds' eggs and butterflies. Here the whole is often greater than the sum of the parts – the room and its contents are indivisible.

The room devoted to the display of china and porcelain is a northern European – specifically Dutch – tradition, dating from the middle of the seventeenth century. Dutch china closets of the 1650s show shelves and brackets used in a conscious attempt to organize and enhance a collection. Towards the end of the seventeenth century, the French architect and furniture designer Daniel Marot (1663–1752), whose concept of the unified interior was so influential in Holland and England, adopted symmetrical arrangements of porcelain on mantelpieces and surrounding fireplaces. In turn, the Delft potteries produced sets of vases in different shapes to form ready-made mantelpiece compositions, known in France as *garnitures de cheminées*. China was also displayed on the gable tops of Dutch armoires, over doors and even in the chimney opening, where in summertime the fireplace might contain a large decorative pot with an orange tree standing in it.

The tops of cabinets, like mantelshelves, were always used for big jars and pots and, in seventeenth-century Holland, for displays of china. These three copper vessels sit on the cabinet cornice like a mantelshelf arrangement. They belong in colour and mass to the piece of furniture, which, in contrast, contains serried ranks of delicate glass and crocheted edgings. Glass is always best seen against a dark background and, of course, should be displayed standing right-way up.

In the 1760s it was fashionable to collect painted china which, even then, was displayed with a strong awareness of colour; china decorated in similar shades was arranged within a room to create a harmonious scheme – a tradition which remains popular today. In the same spirit, blue and white porcelain rooms were a feature of eighteenth-century Swedish decoration. Chinoiserie wall patterns made appropriate backgrounds for these displays and the brackets themselves, in the Rococo style, provided permanent places for the porcelain which was as much decoration as collection.

Being flat, plates have generally been displayed in the same manner as pictures, grouped according to colour or type and hung on the wall. They can, of course, be arranged on the shelves of glass-fronted cabinets or, more humbly, on dressers. In Arts and Crafts interiors of the late-nineteenth century, a collection of willow-pattern plates was often displayed on a deep ledge or shelf two-thirds of the way up the wall – a feature which earned for itself the name of 'Delft rack'.

Statuary has been another longstanding area of interest for the collector. From the Renaissance onwards, relics dug up from classical ruins and the sculpture inspired by such discoveries had found their way into the collections of aristocratic and wealthy patrons.

During the era of the Grand Tour collecting statues, as well as prints, became a fashionable pursuit of young gentlemen. The climax of the tour was a stay in Rome to view the classical ruins and acquire a few mementoes to take home. Some tours were conducted in a spirit of scholarship; others were undertaken in a more lighthearted manner and an entire industry emerged out of the demand for souvenirs and replicas of classical statuary; original antique fragments were often combined to make new 'antique' pieces. In this context, collecting was more a matter of conspicuous consumption than the adjunct of serious study.

Such sculpture and statuary tended to be displayed in galleries or in more inherently architectural settings. Pieces might be arranged on half-columns or plinths, standing in alcoves or niches the length of a gallery; small pieces were sometimes arranged on brackets. Backgrounds were light and 'stony', the architectural detailing resolutely classical. This classical approach to displaying sculpture is essentially static. We look at the collection, but have no contact with it. Plinths and brackets link the pieces with the architecture and our involvement is that of spectators. Of course there have always also been, as well as these grand set pieces, table sculptures and informal groupings of things on shelves and mantelpieces – objects to be touched and moved around. Sculpture also embraces the *objet trouvé* and any collection of such objects will gain in immediacy by such an informal arrangement.

Some things need the protection afforded by being placed on a bracket or, if larger, a plinth. Brackets at their simplest will be no more than shelves, but plaster or resin castings, with perhaps an added shelf on top, are available. Just as important, perhaps even more so, is the placing of these objects, especially if the collection is small. They can help focus attention on a door, window or fireplace, and should bear some relation to the architecture. If the collection is large there may be little or no choice in the placing.

A collection of blue and white plates makes a positive contribution to the decoration while hiding the security grille that disfigures the window. The same treatment could be used to disguise a displeasing view.